Mr. Lincoln's Washington

Mr. Lincoln's Washington

Stanley Preston Kimmel

Coward-McCann, Inc. New York

Books by
Stanley Kimmel

Gen'l (handwritten)

CRUCIFIXION
LEAVES ON THE WATER
THE KINGDOM OF SMOKE
THE MAD BOOTHS OF MARYLAND

Library of Congress Catalog Card Number: 57-12198

MANUFACTURED IN THE UNITED STATES OF AMERICA

Nancy Hanks

If Nancy Hanks
Came back as a ghost,
  Seeking news
Of what she loved most,
  She'd ask first
  "Where's my son?
What's happened to Abe
  What's he done?"

  "Poor little Abe,
  Left all lone
  Except for Tom
Who's a rolling stone;
  He was only nine
  The year I died,
  I remember still
  How hard he cried.

  "Scraping alone
In a little shack
  With hardly a shirt
To cover his back
  And a prairie wind
To blow him down,
  Or pinching dimes
If he went to town.

"You wouldn't know
  About my son?
Did he grow tall?
  Did he have fun?
Did he learn to read?
  Did he go to town?
Do you know his name?
  Did he get on?"

ROSEMARY BENÉT

Foreword

MR. LINCOLN'S WASHINGTON is not an attempt to detail history. It reports local events, selected from Washington newspapers, which Lincoln himself might have read. Reports of national events, and of nearby places, which affected the population of the Capital, and therefore became a part of the local scene, are included.

For photographs, prints, and other illustrations, I am indebted to: National Archives, Library of Congress, National Park Service (Interior Department), Columbia Historical Society, Washingtonian Room of the Washington Public Library, Smithsonian Institution, *Washington Post* and *Washington Evening Star*.

I am grateful to the following members of the above staffs, and others, who assisted in locating this material: Josephine Cobb, Ruth M. King, Josephine Motylewski, Howard Gardner, Joe Thomas, Milton Kaplan, Hirst Milhollen, Carl Stange, Virginia Daiker, Dr. C. Percy Powell, T. Sutton Jett, Cornelius W. Heine, Stanley W. McClure, Carol Smith, Dr. Lawrence F. Schmeckebier, Ethel Lacy, Edith Ray Saul; Rudolph Kauffmann, Jack K. Burness, Mr. and Mrs. Edgar C. Cox of the L.C. Handy Studio, Mrs. Elizabeth Burroughs Kelley, Sargent Virginia Pickel, and Dr. J. T. Dorris.

S.K.

Mr. Lincoln's Washington

A City of Strangers

Sightseers, streetwalkers, gamblers, war-mongers, lobbyists; office-seekers and contract-wranglers mingled with the crowds in downtown Washington as the day for the inauguration of a prairie President drew near.

Mr. Abraham Lincoln, master of wit and wisdom, and political strategy, had arrived in the capital under a cloak of secrecy. Newspapers reported a lively scene at the Baltimore and Ohio Railroad station at New Jersey Avenue and C Street, Northwest, where crowds surged about expecting the President-elect at 4:00 P.M. on Saturday, February 23, 1861.

Sheltered from a drizzling rain, they waited, joked, whistled and swore until five o'clock when Senator William H. Seward of New York, and Congressman Elihu B. Washburne of Illinois arrived and four carriages drove up to the rear car of a special train which had just pulled into the depot. But Mr. Lincoln did not appear. Only Mrs. Lincoln and their three sons, Robert, aged seventeen, William and Thomas, seven and ten years younger than their brother, with other members of the party, passed through a lane kept open by the police. The press described Mrs. Lincoln as having "a comely, matronly, lady-like face, bearing an unmistakable air of goodness, striking the opposite of the ill-natured portraits of her by the pens of some of the sensation letter-writers." As they all drove to Willard's Hotel, "the crowd plunged after them through rain and mud as if determined to escort a presidential party anyhow."

Rumors of a plot to assassinate the President-elect in Baltimore when his special train passed through there, had not been discounted by those in charge of his safety, and he had been brought into Washington on another train at dawn that same morning. But not wearing "a Scotch plaid cap and a very long military cloak, so that he was entirely unrecognizable," as reported. A soft wool hat, given to him by a friend in New York, and an old overcoat which he had with him, had made up the disguise for the last lap of the journey.

As the tall, gaunt Lincoln, whose sad expression was fringed by recently grown whiskers, came from the train, he was accompanied by detective Allan Pinkerton, and stalwart Ward Hill Lamon, who had practiced law with him in Illinois. Lamon also played the banjo and sang Lincoln's favorite folk songs, but he had come with him from Springfield as a sort of bodyguard. Without warning, a man who had been behind a pillar approached Lincoln and said, "You can't play that on me." Immediately Lamon raised his fist to ward off the stranger. "Don't strike him," said Lincoln. "It is Washburne."

First known photograph of Lincoln taken after his arrival in Washington (1861). *Library of Congress.*

11

Willard's Hotel, Fourteen Street and Pennsylvania Avenue, Northwest, where Lincoln and his family occupied rooms until the inauguration. *National Park Service*.

The Baltimore & Ohio railroad station at New Jersey and C Street, Northwest, where Lincoln arrived at dawn on February 23, 1861. *National Park Service*.

Senator William H. Seward of New York. *National Park Service*.

Aware of the change in Lincoln's traveling schedule, the Illinois Congressman was on hand to greet him. All but Pinkerton got into Washburne's carriage and drove to Willard's Hotel where the Lincolns were to stay before moving into the White House, only a short distance up Pennsylvania Avenue. The hotel was known as the meeting place of notables in the political, business, and professional life of the city and nation. It was also the social center, and many public and private affairs for visiting dignitaries were held there.

That wintry day, Mayor James E. Barret and the city's Board of Aldermen came to the parlor Lincoln occupied at the hotel to welcome him with words spoken by the mayor. Lincoln's response did not avoid some remarks on the situation in which he had been placed. After thanking the mayor and the municipal authorities for their friendly greeting, he said:

"And as it is the first time in my life, since the present phase of politics has presented itself in this country, that I have said anything publicly within a region of the country where the institution of slavery exists, I will take this

Mrs. Lincoln and her three sons, Robert, William, and Thomas, at about the time they arrived in Washington. *National Park Service.*

13

Seward's home across from the White House (site of old Belasco Theatre). *National Park Service.*

Washington newspapers were located elsewhere in the northwest part of the city: *The Evening Star* shown above (left), at Eleventh Street and Pennsylvania Avenue, and *The National Intelligencer* at Seventh and D Streets, were the best known. Others included the *National Republican,* and the *Sunday Morning Chronical,* later the *Daily Chronical. Washington Evening Star.*

Newspaper Row, opposite Willard's Hotel on Fourteenth Street, Northwest, showing buildings occupied by the *New York Herald, Tribune, World, Boston Advertiser,* and the *Western Union Telegraph* where correspondents from other cities filed copy. The *New York Times* building is seen in the upper background, and the old Ebbitt House (site of National Press Club) at the far left. *Columbia Historical Society.*

occasion to say that I think very much of the ill feeling that has existed, and still exists, between the people in the sections from whence I came and the people here, is dependent upon a misunderstanding of one another. I therefore avail myself of this opportunity to assure you, Mr. Mayor, and all the gentlemen present, that I have not now, and never have had, any other than as kindly feelings toward you as the people of my own section. I have not now, and never have had, any disposition to treat you in any respect otherwise than as my own neighbors. I have not now any purpose to withhold from you any of the benefits of the Constitution, under any circumstances that I would feel myself constrained to withhold from my own neighbors, and I hope, in a word, that when we shall become better acquainted, and I say it with great confidence, we shall like each other the more."

Surrounded by people, most of whom were friendly, with politicians and delegations waiting to see him, Lincoln took time to worship at St. John's Episcopal Church that first Sunday. With Seward he walked the short distance

St. John's Episcopal Church, near the White House, where Lincoln worshiped the first Sunday after his arrival in Washington. *Washington Public Library.*

Lincoln sitting before a fireplace in Willard's Hotel reading a newspaper on the eve of his inauguration. Drawn by Thomas Nast, one of the newspaper artists covering Washington at this time. *National Park Service.*

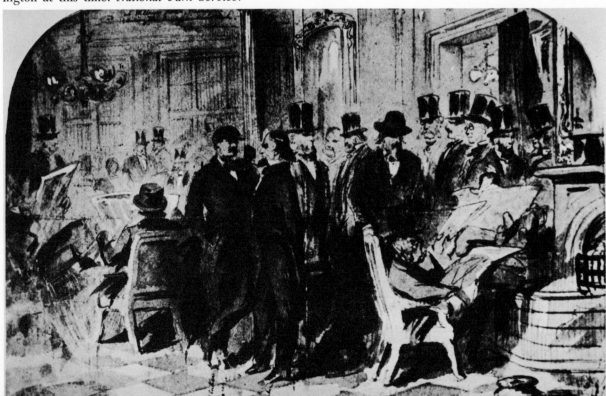

15

from the hotel across Jackson Square to the church, within view of the White House, and occupied Seward's pew near the altar. Most of the congregation and Dr. Pyne, the rector, were unaware of Lincoln's presence. The press described the President-elect as "dressed in plain black clothes, with black whiskers and hair well trimmed, and was pronounced by such as recognized him as a different man entirely from the hard-looking pictorial representations seen of him. Some of the ladies say that in fact he is almost good-looking." From there they went to Seward's home, where they dined, and returned to the hotel later in the afternoon.

That evening, while Lincoln was being serenaded by the Marine Band, a large crowd gathered in front of the hotel and made repeated calls for the President-elect. After several musical pieces had been played, Lincoln appeared at one of the windows and again expressed, in slightly different phrases, the opinions he had given the city's representatives the day before. He wanted the people of Washington to regard him as a friend, he said, and not as someone "narrowly splitting hairs" with them, or intent upon depriving them of the rights they enjoyed under the Constitution of the United States. His words brought hearty cheers from the crowd, and when he had finished, the band played "Yankee Doodle."

The press was now on Lincoln's heels, and throughout the long years to come, life as a private citizen in Springfield, Illinois, would be only a memory. New names were to be set up in type, and days which had been insignificant in other years were to note battles, victories, defeats, deaths. Such possible events surely crowded his mind as he sat before a

16

The Corcoran Art Building.   Franklin School.

Bird's eye view of downtown Washington during the 1860's. To the right, the Old City Canal flows past the unfinished Washington Monument (then 154 feet high), and the Smithsonian Institution which are south of it. One of the bridges crossing the canal is seen about half way between these two points. The

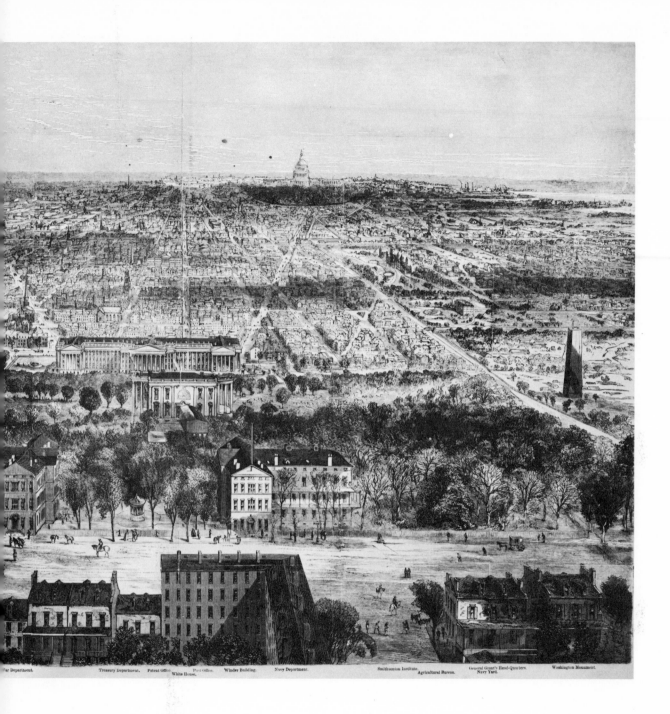

War Department. Treasury Department. Patent Office. Post Office. Winder Building. Navy Department. Smithsonian Institute. Agricultural Bureau. General Grant's Head-Quarters. Washington Monument.
White House. Navy Yard.

President's Park is an extension of the grounds, directly north of the monument and the canal, leading to the White House shown in the center of the drawing. In the foreground west of the White House are the War and the Navy and the State Department buildings. To the left is Lafayette Square, facing the White House, and Pennsylvania Avenue which turns at Fifteenth Street and continues from the Treasury building in a straight line eastward to the Capitol seen in the background. The Patent Office and Interior Department at Seventh and F streets, Judiciary Square, City Hall, County Jail, E Street Infirmary, churches, schools, homes, and the business section of Washington, are in the area at the upper left, north of the Avenue about half way between the Treasury building and the Capitol. At the upper right is the Potomac River.

Library of Congress.

17

Looking east on F Street, Northwest, toward the Patent office building seen in the distance at left. *National Park Service.*

Washington transportation prior to the introduction of street horse cars. *Washington Evening Star.*

fireplace in Willard's Hotel reading a newspaper on the eve of his first inauguration.

There had been few changes in Washington since Lincoln's departure in 1849 after serving one term as a Representative from Illinois. Government buildings were few, most of them widely separated. Travel between them depended mostly upon slow moving hacks and omnibuses, often filled to capacity. The Capitol, with its unfinished dome topped by a huge crane and encircled by scaffolding, blocked the straight line of Pennsylvania Avenue leading eastward from the expanding Treasury Building and the Executive Mansion, as the White House was called. In all, this main thoroughfare of the city was four miles long and one hundred and sixty feet wide. Within

City Hall at Fourth and D Streets, Northwest, showing carriage block at entrance to home across from it. *Library of Congress.*

18

The War and Navy buildings bordering Pennsylvania Avenue as seen from Seventeenth Street, Northwest. *Library of Congress.*

the area north of the avenue were the General Post Office and the unfinished Patent Office, which also housed the Interior Department, at Seventh and F Streets, Northwest, surrounded by homes, schools, and churches bordering the business section. At the southern end of Sixth and Seventh Streets were wharves where river steamboats and sailing vessels arrived and departed. The larger shops, hotels and restaurants were on the north side of the Avenue or nearby in the same vicinity. The south side of the Avenue, except for the Center Market at Ninth Street, was taboo for the elite since brothels and gambling establishments operated more or less openly in this neighborhood. The elite also stayed away from such sections as Swam-

poodle, Negro Hill, and the alley domains inhabited by rabble-rousers, thieves and cutthroats.

On the Potomac River side of this business section stood the Smithsonian Institution with its spacious grounds dotted by growing shrubs and trees. In line with it was the Washington Monument which still had two-thirds of the way to go on its climb upward. Around the bend of the Avenue at Fifteenth Street, Northwest, and slightly beyond the White House, were two brick buildings, one occupied by the War and Navy Departments, the other by the State Department. An iron fence, with large gates, and a bronze statue of Thomas Jefferson ornamented the front lawn of the White House looking across the Avenue to

The State Department building at the corner of Pennsylvania Avenue and Fifteenth Street, Northwest. *Library of Congress.*

The old City Canal, described as a fetid bayou filled with floating dead cats, all kinds of putridity, and reeking with pestilential odors. *National Park Service.*

Lafayette Square and the bronze statue of Andrew Jackson riding a prancing steed. Directly back of the White House was the President's Park bordered by marshlands which bred mosquitoes and malaria during the humid summer months. On the outer fringes of the city, southeast to west of the Capitol, were the Navy Yard and Marine Barracks, the Arsenal and Penitentiary on Greenleaf's Point where the Eastern Branch met the Potomac River, and the heights of Georgetown.

To the multitude of strangers then in the capital, and to residents also, Washington was not the most popular city in the Union. Its limited supply of water endangered any building swept by fire and also the lives of those who drank it. Along the south edge of the Mall, extending the length of the Avenue from the Capitol to the rear of the White House and the river, slowly crept the Old City Canal, described as a fetid bayou filled with floating dead cats, all kinds of putridity and reeking with pestilential odors. Crossing the iron

bridges, which linked the two sections of the city, was not a pleasant undertaking. Cattle, swine, sheep, geese, ran at large everywhere. "Happy hogs" wallowed in the gutters. Only two short sewers served the entire city, and they were so clogged that their contents backed into cellars and stores on the Avenue.

Streets had "no pretense of pavement." Cobblestones were so unstable as to be worse than none at all. On wet days Pennsylvania Avenue was a river of mud and filth. Even carts and light buggies often were mired down. During the dry season, dust obliterated vehicles and pedestrians alike.

"What most is needed to contribute to the comfort and pleasure of citizens and strangers?" asked the press. "The removal of mud and dust! This nuisance is the curse of Washington. It is as annoying as the flies of Egypt. It penetrates everywhere. It fills our carriages; it enters our houses; it spoils our clothes; it blinds our eyes; it injures our lungs; it frets our temper; it drives away strangers; in fine, it is the great plague of our lives. . . ." It was "a constant joke," that real estate was high in dry weather, as it was, for the most part, all in the air.

"That the plan of our city is a most unfortunate one . . . every resident will be ready to admit and deeply regret. The streets are almost universally too wide, affording unnecessary space for the accumulation of dust, but when we add to these our immense avenues, from one hundred and sixty to two hundred feet wide—a great Sahara of dirt—the blunder of the plan is seen to be prodigious. If the space thus worse than wasted had been laid out in numerous small squares, which could be planted with trees and kept in grass, it would have been a great improvement."

URDAY, March 2d, at 7 o'clock p. m. A full meeting is desired upon important business.
By order of the Captain:
mar 1 2t*   JOHN HICKY. Sec.

☞ DUST, DUST, DUST.—NOTICE—All persons doing business on Penn. avenue are requested to meet in the room over Galt & Bro.'s Jewelry Store, on SATURDAY EVENING, 2d inst., at 7½ o'clock, to adopt some plan for scraping and watering the avenue.   ma 1 2t

☞ UNIVERSALISM—Rev. John M. Austin, editor of the New York Christian Ambassador, one of the most talented Clergymen in

Item in Washington *Evening Star*, two days before the inauguration, calls attention to dust, dust, dust. *Washington Evening Star*.

Pennsylvania Avenue, 1861: a desert of dust during the dry season and a sea of mud when rain fell upon it. Everyone complained about it and denounced city officials for not improving the main thoroughfare of the city. The unfinished dome of the Capitol is seen in the distance. *National Park Service*.

President James Buchanan. *National Archives.*

It was not without reason that Washington was called "a city of magnificent distances." The press suggested that the City Council "awake to their duty" and have the thoroughfares most traveled between the Capitol and the White House promptly paved as an example of exterminating the nuisance of mud and dust.

"This important day of March, 1861," wrote a reporter on the fourth of that month, "dawned rather inauspiciously with leaden skies, and tornadoes of dust, which was leveled somewhat later by a slight fall of rain. As the morning wore on, however, the skies brightened and the wind lulled, auguries noted with some complacence by those who pin their faith upon such omens. The streets thus early were crammed with pedestrians, ninety-

Mr. Lincoln on his way to the Capitol, to be inaugurated. *National Park Service.*

nine faces out of one hundred being those of
strangers. The crowd in this city is undoubtedly larger by half than on any previous occasion of the sort, but the proportion of ladies
is very much smaller. Of these arrivals it is
safe to say that two-thirds are Western men."

Early in the forenoon the neighborhood of
Willard's Hotel was filled with excited people,
all waiting to get a glimpse of the President-
elect. They seemed to be in a very good
humor, according to reports, "except when
some official trespassed on what they considered their reserve rights, when they did not
hesitate to damn them to an unlimited extent.
About 11 o'clock the military formed, and the
hotel presented an animated appearance,
every window being crowded. A little after
12 o'clock the word was passed along the line
of infantry on the Avenue and the cavalry on
Fourteenth Street, to present arms. This was
handsomely done when the President and
President-elect emerged from the lower (Fourteenth Street) door of the hotel. They were
warmly applauded, and from our position in
front of the crowd, we heard not a single remark offensive to the outgoing or incoming
President. This argues well for the self respect
of our citizens. Mr. Buchanan looked, as usual,
dignified and at his ease, and Mr. Lincoln
seemed to bear his honors meekly, and to be
not at all excited by the surging, swaying
crowd which surrounded him. Mr. Buchanan's
private carriage was first drawn up to the entrance, but from what we could learn of the
movements going on we judge that the President-elect preferred to make his appearance
in an open carriage, where all could see him,
as one was substituted for Mr. Buchanan's
closed carriage.

"The President and President-elect took
their seats in the carriage, the military at a
'present arms' and the band on the left [Ma-
rine Band directed by Francis Scala] playing
'Hail To The Chief'. Senator James A. Pearce
(Maryland), and Senator Edward D. Baker
(Oregon), of the committee arrangements,
having been seated in the same carriage, it
moved out to its position in the line, being
preceded by the company of Sappers and
Miners, and flanked on the right by the

Francis Scala, leader of the Marine band which
played at all important functions in the Capital and
often gave concerts on the White House grounds.
U.S. Defense Department (*Marine Corps*).

Crowd gathering at the Capitol for Lincoln's first
inauguration. *National Park Service*.

23

The third house from the right in this row of buildings directly east of the Capitol (site of Library of Congress) was once the boarding house of a Mrs. Spriggs where Lincoln lived while a Congressman from Illinois (1847-1848).

Banner used in political campaign showing Lincoln without whiskers. *National Park Service.*

Georgetown Mounted Guard, and on the left by the President's Mounted Guard. There was some grumbling at this arrangement, as it was almost impossible to get a view of the President-elect, which seemed to be the chief object in view with the majority of the spectators."

Thousands of citizens, in carriages, on horseback, and on foot, thronged the route over which they passed while others awaited their arrival at the Capitol. Headed by Major William H. French, Marshal in Chief, the long line of march included various political delegations, members of Congress, the diplomatic corps, governors of the states, soldiers, sailors, marines, and a score of dignitaries. Among the floats was one provided by Republicans of the city decorated and furnished to allegorize the Constitution and the Union, the states and territories represented by a corresponding number of little girls dressed in white. It was drawn by six horses partly covered with trappings on which was printed in large letters the word UNION.

Several floats carried banners, used in the political campaign, showing a man who did not resemble the President-elect in the carriage. Since Lincoln had grown a beard shortly before leaving Springfield not everyone had been aware of the change in his features. As the procession approached the Capitol grounds, Lincoln passed within view of Ann Spriggs' boarding house at Pennsylvania Avenue and First Street, Northeast, where he had lived when a congressman from Illinois in 1847-1848, and witnessed the traffic in slaves in that neighborhood.

"Inauguration time," observed a reporter, "inevitably brings to this city a number of oddish people, some decidedly crazy, and some about half and half. Where they burrow during the four years interval we know not, but as soon as Inauguration Day comes around, they are on hand here, bristling with eccentricities and idiosyncrasies."

A slave market such as Lincoln saw from the windows of the Capitol while a member of Congress. *National Park Service.*

The inaugural procession passing the gate of the Capitol grounds. *Library of Congress.*

Upon arrival at the Capitol, Lincoln and Buchanan entered the north wing and went to the Senate chamber to witness the swearing in of Hannibal Hamlin, the new Vice President. The above sketch from Harper's Weekly shows them entering the Senate chamber. *National Park Service.*

While the procession was on its way to the Capitol, another "inaugural address" was being spoken according to the reporter. "A little man in large red whiskers, and dressed in travel-stained attire, who had been lounging about the edges of the crowd for some time, mounted into one of the tall trees in front of the east portico and, selecting a strong and convenient branch, he perched himself upon it, and drawing a package of manuscript from his pocket began with many oratorical flourishes to deliver an address to the crowd below. His eccentric and somewhat perilous gyrations attracted the attention of the several thousand spectators there assembled, all of whom awaited to see him tumble headlong.

"What his speech amounted to no one could tell, beyond the fact that it appeared to be a discursive homily upon the vices of the times. Several persons, among whom was a special policeman, mounted into the tree to bring down the ambitious lecturer, and the policeman being a first rate climber led the van, and got so near as to grasp the crazy man by the foot, when he, looking down and seeing his danger, mounted nimbly into the very topmost branches of the tree, far out of the reach of those in pursuit. Here he ensconced himself, the little branches swaying to and fro with his weight, and resumed his lecture, which he concluded to his own satisfaction, and then kindly distributed the manuscript among the audience. He then pulled out a package of tracts, which he bestowed upon those who were nearest and could seize upon them. By this time his pursuers had given up the chase and returned to terra firma, where they awaited his descent. After bestowing a fatherly benediction upon his hearers, the lecturer descended with great dignity to the ground, where he was instantly captured, and ignominiously marched off between two specials to the Capitol guardhouse."

Upon arrival at the Capitol, Lincoln and Buchanan entered the North Wing and went

The east front of the Capitol, with its dome and wing still under construction, and described as resembling a Roman ruin, was the scene of the inaugural ceremonies. *National Park Service.*

to the Senate Chamber to witness the swearing in of Hannibal Hamlin, the new Vice President. Then they passed to the east front of the Capitol, with its dome and wing still under construction, and described as resembling a Roman ruin, for the inaugural ceremonies. The Oath of Office was administered by Chief Justice Roger B. Taney, then eighty-four years old, and the Bible on which Lincoln, the sixteenth President of the United States, placed his hand was held by a black-robed barrister. On a platform erected over the main steps, and under a canopy "to protect the President-elect from possible rain," Abraham Lincoln read his first inaugural address. He spoke "with a clear, loud, and distinct voice, quite intelligible by at least ten thousand persons below him, who gave repeated and hearty applause to the sentiments uttered." In closing he said:

"In your hands, my dissatisfied fellow-

Hannibal Hamlin. *National Park Service.*

The oath of office was administrated by Chief Justice Roger B. Taney, then eighty-four years old. *National Park Service.*

Mathew Brady, who became famous for his photographs of the Civil War period, took his first view of the White House in 1861. The bronze statue of Thomas Jefferson was later removed to the Rotunda in the Capitol. *National Park Service.*

General Winfield Scott. "Old fuss and feathers" they called him. *National Archives.*

countrymen, and not in mine, is the momentous issue of civil war. The Government will not assail you. You can have no conflict without being yourselves the aggressors. You have no oath registered in Heaven to destroy the Government, while I shall have the most solemn one to preserve, protect, and defend it. I am loath to close. We are not enemies, but friends. We must not be enemies. Though passions may have strained, it must not break our bonds of affection. The mystic chords of memory, stretching from every battle-field and patriot grave to every living heart and hearth-stone, all over this broad land, will yet swell the chorus of the Union, when again touched, as surely they will be, by the better angles of our nature."

After the Marine Band had played a new National song with the prophetic title, "God

30

Probably one of the first Brady photographs of Lincoln as president. *National Park Service.*

A portrait of Mary Todd Lincoln painted by Katherine Helm at the time of the first inauguration. *National Park Service.*

Save Our President," written and set to music by two Washington residents for this special occasion, Lincoln, Hamlin, and members of their party drove to the White House. The only disturbances during the inaugural ceremonies were made by those in the crowd who discovered that the light-fingered gentry were operating among them and called for the police who picked up a score of pickpockets. Reports in the local columns were similar: "Mr. Joseph Aldrich, of this city, had his wallet stolen from his pantaloons pocket, and with it seven or eight dollars in gold and silver."

At the White House Lincoln found the towering General-in-chief of the United States Army, Winfield Scott, waiting to greet him; also a crowd numbered at thousands, who, when doors were thrown open, rapidly passed through the reception room, pausing a moment to shake hands with the President. Lincoln appeared in excellent spirits, and gave each visitor a cordial handclasp, often speaking a few words to someone whom he recognized.

That evening the Union Inauguration Ball (as advertised) was held in the White Muslin Palace of Aladdin, a large hall on Judiciary Square. Under an array of white and blue muslin decorations and the light of gas chandeliers, the President and Mayor Barret led the Grand March with Mrs. Lincoln and Senator Stephen A. Douglas of Illinois close behind them. As they danced few realized the precautions that had been taken. "Old Fuss and Feathers", as General Scott was known, had vowed to defend the capital and the President against all enemies including "hell

Soldiers guarding the white Muslin Palace of Aladdin on the night of the first inaugural ball. *Library of Congress.*

Grand inaugural ball in honor of the President and Mrs. Lincoln at the White Muslin Palace of Aladdin erected behind the City Hall for this occasion. *Library of Congress.*

and high water"—and he did. Soldiers and cannons guarded the rear of the building, alerted for quick action in any direction should that be necessary. Many of those attending were said to have been residents of the Northern and Western states.

One of these, Edward P. Weston, was a young pedestrian from Boston who had walked from that city to Washington in payment of an election debt lost when Lincoln won. He had arrived in the capital on the previous evening wearing blue woolen knit drawers, fitted tightly to his limbs, and a blue coat with brass buttons. He was tired, sore, and weak, and declared he would not undertake a journey again over such roads for any amount of money. He said "the committee of two" who had accompanied him had worn out three horses along the way, and that one man had been compelled to finish the trip by train from Annapolis Junction. "Probably he will be careful how he bets next time," said a wag who had seen him at the Inaugural Ball with the Massachusetts delegation.

Other visitors were also in the city. A newspaper of that date advertised:

NEGROES WANTED—The subscriber wishes to purchase, for his own use on his cotton plantation in Rapides parish, Louisiana, a stock of from twenty to fifty good Negroes, in which there shall be a fair proportion of serviceable men. Any person having such to dispose of will please to address me, enclosing fully descriptive list, care of Box No. 282 post office, city of Washington, until 15th March.
G. Mason Graham

There were departures too. On the afternoon following the Ball, ex-President Buchanan left Washington on his journey to his home in Wheatland, Pennsylvania, where he spent the remainder of his life in retirement. He was escorted to the railroad station by the President's Mounted Guard, numbering sixty-five of the rank and file, and the first battalion of the Union Regiment, commanded by Major J. T. Jewell. As the train left, "three hearty cheers" were given for the ex-President. "What provoked the cheers was quite a mystery, except to those glad to be rid of him," remarked an Abolitionist who had watched the demonstration.

The President's first Levee must have given the new occupants of the White House some idea of what was in store for them on such occasions. "A crowd was anticipated," wrote one reporter, "but we suppose few expected *quite* such a jam, after an adjournment of Congress. So dense was the pressure that hundreds, after Herculean efforts to worm their way through the throng, gave it up in despair, and went home without seeing the new President."

For more than two and one-half hours Lincoln stood shaking the hands of some three thousand persons who greeted him. At his left was Ward Hill Lamon, at his right were Mrs. Lincoln and the ladies of her party numbering several relatives. "Mr. Lincoln," observed the reporter, "was dressed in black, with white gloves, turndown collar, and with his luxuriant black hair parted down the middle. Mrs. Lincoln wore a rich, bright crimson watered silk, with point lace cape, white and red camelias in her hair, pearl band and necklace, and other ornaments of pearl." To one man in the crowd, Lincoln (six feet and four inches tall) said he allowed no human being taller than himself to go unchallenged. The man answered that his family name was Hatcher, that he came from Virginia, and was six feet and seven inches tall.

"The last scene of the Levee was a tragic one," continued the reporter. "The mob of coats, hats, and caps left in the hall had somehow got inextricably mixed up and misappropriated, and perhaps not one in ten of that large assemblage emerged with the same outer garments they wore on entering. Some thieves seem to have taken advantage of the opportunity to make a grand sweep, and a very good business they must have done. Some of the victims, utterly refusing to don the greasy, kinky apologies for hats left on hand, tied up their heads in handkerchiefs and so wended their way sulkily homeward."

The following day newspapers carried a host of items under LOST AND FOUND:
"LOST—Last night, at the President's Levee, a black ribbed cloth overcoat, with velvet collar and facings. The finder will confer a favor on the owner by leaving it at No. 324 5th st. be-

Two advertisements which appeared in a Washington newspaper during the first month of Lincoln's administration. Apparently the Negro was not returned, and Clark Mills, sculptor who designed the equestrian statue of General Andrew Jackson in Lafayette Square, was trying to hire another one. Note the figure of a Negro running away which was often used in such advertisements, and other items which refer to events that month. *Washington Evening Star.*

tween I and K sts; or at the marble works, corner New York av. and Fifteen st. Thos. H. Dorean.

"Found—Taken by mistake, in the scramble at the Levee last night, a black cloth overcoat, containing papers doubtless of some value to the owner. It has been left at this office for exchange.

"Notice—If the gentleman who took an overcoat from the Levee last night will return the papers in the breast pocket belonging to Thomas Hill of Sacramento, Calif., either through the Post office or directed to the undersigned at 332 Twelfth st., he will be welcome to the overcoat and receive the thanks of its owner, Thomas Fitch.

"Taken by Mistake—at the President's Levee last night, an overcoat containing a letter, some visiting cards and handkerchief. The owner can have the coat by calling at 404 E st., north, proving property and paying for this advertisement. Also lost same night, same place, a black broadcloth overcoat, velvet collar, lower button off on left hand side, a net worsted cap in pocket. Any person having a coat answering this description will confer

a favor by leaving it at 404 E street north, between 9th and 10th sts."

Another item headed "an impudent stranger" appeared a few days later under Local News—For several days past, a woman has been constantly annoying families in the Seventh Ward by her cool impudence. No one knows her, or where she hails from. She roves from place to place, and when meal time comes, she enters the first house at hand, takes her seat at the table, and helps herself. She has been ejected from several houses, but not arrested, no one wishing to complain, supposing her a lunatic. Recently, however, the loss of various small articles immediately after her visits occasioned the belief that she is not exactly a lunatic, but a passing thief of considerable nerve. She is a short, stout woman, about thirty years of age."

Also on that date, newspapers advertised:

Lincoln as he is.
    Steel Engraved Portrait.
  The best Portrait yet published of
Hon. Abraham Lincoln, (*with whiskers,*)
  At French & Richstein's,
    No. 278 Penna. Avenue,
      Washington, D. C.
Trade supplied at low prices.   mar 7

Many persons, having purchased photographs or drawings of Lincoln when nominated, expecting him to be the next President, now had to replace them with likenesses showing him "with whiskers."

With parades, quadrilles, and the inauguration behind them, Washington began to hear the drum-beats of events to come. United States troops, numbering some six hundred fifty soldiers, had been ordered to the city to act in strict obedience to the civil authorities and the police in preserving peace and order. No resident of Washington could scan his daily newspaper, nor converse with his neighbor, without realizing that the powder-keg upon which the nation sat was dangerously near to explosion.

The Peace Convention, in session at the Concert Hall of Willard's Hotel when Lincoln arrived, was a broken bubble. Ex-President

THE COMING MAN'S PRESIDENTIAL CAREER, à la BLONDIN.
Motto.——Don't Give up the Ship.

Another cartoon of Lincoln without whiskers which portrayed him as the famous tightrope walker crossing Niagara Falls. *Library of Congress.*

John Tyler had presided over the delegates from twenty-one states in an effort to prevent secession. Made up of old men, it had tottered down the gangplank of dissension and into a sea of political oblivion. "What good could be expected from such a conference?" cried Southern sympathizers in Washington.

Then, in April, local newspapers blazed with reports of a CONFLICT AT CHARLESTON. Telegraphic dispatches described the bombardment of Fort Sumter by Confederate batteries in command of General Pierre G. T. Beauregard. The demand that Major Robert Anderson and his Federal troops evacuate the fort had been declined. "We opened fire at 4:30" (A.M.) read Beauregard's communication of April 12 to L. P. Walker, Confederate Secretary of War. Two days later the fort was in their hands.

News of the siege and surrender was discussed by everyone in Washington. People gathered in hotel lobbies and other public places to compare views of the event. Many believed that the reports of surrender were one-sided and unreliable, since the capture of a fort said to be so strong and complete as

The advance of Union troops in defense of the city of Washington. *National Archives.*

Sumter was effected in so short a time and without casualties. Some justified the surrender on the ground that Major Anderson was without provisions, had less than sixty men with him, and that he neither received, nor could have expected, any co-operation from the Federal fleet off Charleston Harbor. A few expressed distrust of all news relating to the affair, and believed that it was designed only to effect the decision of Virginia with reference to leaving or continuing in the Union.

"It is true to say that deep interest was manifested, but we saw little or nothing of what is called 'excitement,'" a reporter confessed. Even Joseph Jefferson, the popular thirty-two-year-old comedian, played before a full house that evening at the Washington Theatre, on the corner of C and Eleventh Streets, Northwest, taking the role of Caleb Plummer in *The Cricket On The Hearth*.

But the war, which no one wanted, except those able to profit by it, and no one had been able to prevent, had begun. And in Washington, Lincoln came to his first great decision as President, and the signing of his first notable document: a proclamation calling 75,000 men to suppress obstruction of Federal Laws in the secession states of South Carolina, Georgia, Alabama, Florida, Mississippi, Louisiana, and Texas, and to summon Congress to the capital on July 4 for the purpose of considering and determining such measures as the public safety and interest of the Nation demanded.

Offers of aid to the Federal Government poured into Washington from states supporting the Union. Arms, men, money, and railroads were placed at the disposal of those whose duty it was to protect national integrity. The Pennsylvania Central Railroad offered the use of its entire equipment for moving Government troops and provisions to the temporary exclusion of all other traffic. Carloads of militia and supplies arrived daily, and the grounds facing the War Department near the White House became a recruiting camp. Enlistments swelled the corps of various military groups already established in the city—the Metropolitan Rifles, the Hender-

Troops drilling in the grounds on the north side of the Capitol. *National Park Service*.

Bird's-eye view of Sixth Street wharf where military supplies were received. *Library of Congress*.

son Guards, and Captain Kelly's Company among them. Troops drilled in the grounds on the north side of the Capitol, artillery practiced maneuvers in the open spaces near the Washington Monument, and Marines paraded along streets outside their barracks.

Advertisements appeared in local newspapers for items featuring the national emblem. "A very pretty envelope," one read, "bearing an impression of the flowing flag of the Union in all its colors, has been gotten up by Mr. Casimir Bohm, and will be found on sale by him."

Excitement arose as to what Virginia might do if the conflict spread. Groups of people, gazing toward Alexandria, across the Potomac from Washington, speculated on what might happen to their own security should the river-town fall into Confederate hands. That the ever-rising tide of heated controversy was certain to spill blood at some point along the way to open rebellion came when the Sixth Regiment of Massachusetts arrived in the capital with reports of having been attacked as they passed through Baltimore. They had been clubbed and stoned by a mob that had sought to block their passage by placing heavy objects across several streets. Having failed, the mob resorted to firearms, and the skirmish which followed had left its toll of dead and wounded.

For a time Washington became isolated from the North by the cutting of rail and telegraph communications, and mails from all directions, except for a portion of the West, were interrupted. Freight stoppage cut off food supplies and prices soared. Some residents made heavy bank withdrawals and were

Washington National Intelligencer.

General view of the Potomac River looking toward Alexandria, Virginia, showing the unfinished Washington Monument, as sketched by A. Waud, a newspaper artist, from the roof of the Willard Hotel. *Washington Evening Star*

Arrival of the New York Seventy-first Regiment at the railroad depot in Washington. *National Park Service.*

ready to leave the city. Fear of fleeing customers prompted merchants to collect debts in full. One advertised: "During these warlike times it is all important that persons should pay their bills as speedily as possible; I therefore request that all my customers, in any way indebted to me, will call and settle without delay."

Preparations for the defense of Washington, and the daily arrival of troops, added to the problem of city authorities. The carrying of firearms resulted in many accidents and shooting affairs. Volunteers who seemed to enjoy payday as a pleasant episode in the life of a soldier were advised not "to spend a crown out of a sixpence a day" (more money than they were earning), and to obey all army regulations.

The 69th New York Regiment barracked at Georgetown during the Civil War. *National Park Service.*

With the secession of Virginia, the Confederate flag flew over Alexandria but federal troops commanded the river. Military camps were established on the outskirts of the District. Troops were barracked in Georgetown and a signal camp was set up on Georgetown Heights. In addition, United States infantry, cavalry, and artillery were stationed on the Virginia side of the Long Bridge where roads led southward, and planks were removed to prevent the enemy from charging across the river at that point. Chain Bridge, leading to

View of Georgetown from the Virginia side of the Potomac River. *Columbia Historical Society.*

The south end of the Long Bridge (Fourteenth Street Bridge) with planks removed to prevent rebel cavalry from charging over it. The Capitol is visible at right. *National Archives.*

The Chain Bridge west of Georgetown derived its name from the large chains of a suspension bridge at the same location prior to the Civil War. It was replaced by a wooden bridge, shown above being guarded by Union soldiers. *Library of Congress.*

Georgetown, also was well guarded. Five hundred soldiers guarded the Treasury Building where sandbags were piled high at entrances and barricades set up inside. Here the President and his Cabinet were to take quarters if the rebels attacked Washington and a final stand had to be made by federal troops. The White House, and other public buildings of

importance also were under the watchful eyes of sentries. Cassius Marcellus Clay, friend of Lincoln, and adept with a Bowie knife, rounded up some 300 volunteers to guard the White House and patrol nearby streets. The city braced itself for a possible onslaught, and talk in public places reached such a high pitch of excitement that Mayor Barret issued

Treasury Department Building at Fifteenth Street and Pennsylvania Avenue, North-west, showing the side entrance to the State Department Building (at right) later replaced by an extension of the Treasury.

Barricade in the Treasury Build-ing where the President and his Cabinet were to take quarters if the rebels attacked Wash-ington and a final stand had to be made by federal troops. *National Park Service.*

Cooking and eating arrangements in the courtyard of the Treasury Building. *Washington Public Library.*

a proclamation cautioning all citizens to guard their conduct so there would be no breach of the peace.

The influx of more troops began to tax local housing to the limit. Many of Cassius Clay's volunteers were quartered in the East Room of the White House. Their determined vigilance often invaded the privacy of the President's family, and Captain Lockwood Todd, a cousin of Mrs. Lincoln, had to keep a watchful eye on them. Some 7,500 soldiers were quartered in the Capitol, City Hall, Post Of-

fice, Patent Office, and the Treasury buildings. These were to be the centers of defense against rebel attacks upon the city, and provisions, including barrels of flour, were stored in the basement of each building. Several large frame structures were erected to provide shelter for the overflow and facilities to carry out their command. Warehouses, stables, harness shops, blacksmith shops, also were constructed for army use, and many private homes, including that of Senator Stephen Douglas, were converted into hospitals. The

The Cassius M. Clay Battalion. Citizens defending the White House in April 1861. Lincoln with his Cabinet are in the center. Mrs. Lincoln is in the third second-story window at the left. The photograph was first published by Dr. J. T. Dorris, in his story "Old Cane Springs."

Captain Lockwood Todd, cousin of Mrs. Lincoln, with Willie and Tad Lincoln. *National Park Service*.

private art gallery of banker-millionaire W. W. Corcoran, at Seventeenth Street and Pennsylvania Avenue, Northwest, was taken over by the army quartermaster, and the grounds south of the White House became a pasture for cattle waiting to be slaughtered in the space surrounding the unfinished Washington Monument. Parades, reviews, military drills, and the induction of entire groups of men into the Union army collectively, became everyday affairs.

The famed Colonel E. E. Ellsworth's regiment of New York Fire Zouaves, numbering 1,100 men, were thus sworn into the federal service, declaring it their intention to defend the Union, come what may. The dashing ex-

The Corcoran Art Gallery was taken over by the Army for its clothing department during the Civil War. The building, at Seventeenth Street and Pennsylvania Avenue, Northwest, is still used by the government. *Washington Evening Star.*

GENERAL THOMAS SWEARING IN THE VOLUNTEERS CALLED INTO THE SERVICE OF THE UNITED STATES AT WASHINGTON, D. C.

General George H. Thomas swearing in volunteers in front of the War Department Building. *Washington Public Library*.

Cattle grazing on the White Lot, so called because of a fence painted white which was at the southern end of the White House grounds. It was across from the Washington Monument grounds where cattle was slaughtered for Army beef. The canal, now Constitution Avenue, Northwest, is seen in the lower foreground and the Treasury Building at upper left. *Library of Congress*.

Eighth Massachusetts Regiment quartered in the Capitol rotunda beside scaffolding used in the construction of the dome. *National Park Service.*

ploits of the French Zouaves in the Crimean War had attracted the attention of all light infantry tacticians in the army, and among the regiments formed to resemble them in appearance, were these outstanding troops. Their striking and gay uniforms, with flowing pants, open blue jackets, and natty headgear (they often wore crimson skull caps with blue tassels), drew more than ordinary attention. Ellsworth, a favorite of Lincoln, had arrived in Washington with the family on the special

train from Springfield, and taken over the task of recruiting, organizing, and training these men for the service.

Their first duty, however, was to save Willard's Hotel from fire on the night of May 9. When discovered, Colonel Ellsworth ordered one hundred of his men to assist in extinguishing the flames, but almost the entire regiment jumped from the windows, scaled lightning rods, and performed all sorts of acrobatic stunts. For want of a ladder, two Zouaves

Sleeping bunks of the First
Rhode Island Regiment in the
Patent Office Building, *National
Archives*.

Barrels of flour being rolled into the basement under the Senate Chamber, and the
government bakery under the Capitol. *National Park Service*.

held another from the eaves, while he, with his head down, played water into the burning building. In two hours they had succeeded in saving the entire structure. The Willard brothers, according to reports, "treated them handsomely."

The city seemed to be on a spree. Large Union flags were donated by organizations for use in prominent places. The pageant of gold braid and notables thronging the capital was the motive for a score of receptions given by the President. At one of these, Major Robert Anderson, was hailed for his gallantry at Fort Sumter. By this time the White House was overflowing with office-seekers, contract-wranglers and strangers having only personal

Colonel Elmer E. Ellsworth, a favorite of Lincoln, who recruited, organized, and trained the New York Fire Zouaves for service in the Union Army. *Library of Congress.*

Ellsworth's Zouaves. *National Archives.*

The New York Fire Zouaves save Willard's Hotel. *Library of Congress*.

Office-seekers at Washington who are ready, like good patriots, to serve their country, are all original Lincoln men. 'Tis true, they voted for Pierce and Buchanan, but this was a deep game to insure the election of Lincoln. Cartoon in Harper's Weekly, March 1861. *National Park Service.*

gains to pursue. Of office-seekers Lincoln said that he "felt like a man letting rooms at one end of his house, while the other end was on fire."

In the midst of all these events, one man had left the capital with a heavy heart. He was Colonel Robert E. Lee, who had resigned his commission in the United States Army and was on his way to Richmond, Virginia, leaving his wife at Arlington House to dismantle their home and follow him later. Before she had finished doing so, federal troops began occupying the surrounding territory, and she was forced to go. Their remaining possessions were taken to the Patent Office or carried away by unknown persons.

Southern views relating to the threatened attack on Washington, and quoted by newspapers in the northern capital, were not all of the same opinion. The *Charleston Mercury*

East front of Robert E. Lee's home in Arlington, Virginia, overlooking the Capitol, after Union soldiers occupied the grounds surrounding it. *National Archives.*

protested against the advice of certain other Confederate journals which urged immediate assault on the city and its occupation as the Capital of the Confederate States. "If Washington was offered to us for nothing," said the *Mercury,* "the offer should be rejected. With a new Republic we should have a new Capital, erected in the heart of the South. Let Washington remain, with its magnificent buildings crumbling into ruin, a striking monument to future ages of the folly and wickedness of the people of the North. It would teach a lesson, in its silence and desolation, all the nations of the earth should learn and understand."

Nevertheless, Washington residents continued to live in fear and anxiety that an assault might come from the Confederate army by way of Virginia. Late in May, 1861, news that the Federal Government was de-

tailing some troops in the city for the occupation of Alexandria and the heights on the right bank of the Potomac opposite Washington, added to the excitement. Talk also centered on the report that a number of regiments had been ordered to prepare for service in the field, and that "the storm was about to burst."

The fact that such contemplated military movements by federal troops had been put into effect was announced by the ringing of "alarm bells" in Alexandria. During the night the Advance Guard of the Grand Army and other troops, including Colonel Ellsworth's New York Fire Zouaves, crossed the Long Bridge over the Potomac into Virginia. Confederate sentries fired on them but Ellsworth marched his men to the center of Alexandria and took possession of the town. Rebel officers and soldiers were captured and their military equipment was seized. The United States flag

The advance guard of the Grand Army of the United States crossing the Long Bridge over the Potomac, at 2 A.M. on May 24, 1861. *Washington Public Library.*

Murder of Colonel Ellsworth, and the revenge killing of his assassin, James W. Jackson, by Corporal Francis E. Brownell of the New York Fire Zouaves. *Library of Congress.*

was hoisted to the top of the flagstaff, and Ellsworth, with part of his command, marched to the telegraph office and placed it under guard to prevent news of federal troop movements being sent south of the city.

While there, he discovered the Confederate flag waving over the nearby Marshall House. With a squad of men, he went to the building and requested the proprietor, James W. Jackson, to haul it down. His refusal to do so resulted in Ellsworth and his squad going to the top of the building and attending to the matter. As he descended the stairs, the young colonel was killed by Jackson who fired one load of a double-barrel gun into his heart. Instantly, Corporal Francis E. Brownell, one of Ellsworth's men who had followed him, discharged the contents of his musket into Jackson's brain, and bayoneted his body as it fell.

Fearing open warfare, the Zouaves were ordered not to avenge Ellsworth's assassination by other acts and his body was brought back to Washington. In the uniform of his regiment, it was viewed by thousands as it lay in state in the East Room of the White House. Flags at halfmast and the tolling of bells paid tribute to the gallant young officer over whom Lincoln sobbed, "My boy, my boy, was it necessary this sacrifice should be made?"

At the close of the funeral service, attended by the President and Mrs. Lincoln, Secretary of State William H. Seward, General Winfield Scott, and other notables, the metallic coffin, enveloped in the United States flag, was placed in a hearse drawn by four white horses, and taken to the railroad station for its journey to Ellsworth's home in New York State. As the procession moved along Pennsylvania Avenue with the regiment of Zouaves, unarmed and marching by fours as mourners, other troops

54

stood with uncovered heads, and with thousands of spectators saw Brownell walking in line and carrying the captured Confederate flag "crimson with the colonel's blood."

Evidence of the consideration given to soldiers quartered in Washington was acknowledged in local newspapers. "The patients connected with the Seventy-first Regiment hospital," one read, "take pleasure in returning their most sincere thanks for the many kindnesses so liberally extended to us by the ladies of the neighborhood. We have left behind us those who would rejoice to be near us in our temporary absence from home. Mothers, wives, and sisters are constantly thinking of us. For them to know that, notwithstanding we are among strangers, the kind hand and noble heart of woman have been actively engaged in providing for us many delicacies, so palatable and tempting to the sick, will be to them a source of the most unalloyed pleasure. They have already been apprised of your generosity, Good Ladies, and once more we thank you, hoping that health, happiness, and prosperity will forever dwell in your households."

The youth of the city also joined in efforts contributing to the welfare of Union soldiers. Pupils of the Female Department of the First District School devoted the money usually spent for their annual picnic to buying material for havelocks to be made for volunteers in the Union army. This cloth covering for a military cap, with a flap hanging down on all sides but the front, was worn to protect the soldier from the sun. The President, and members of the Cabinet too, boosted the morale of the troops by visiting nearby camps and cheering soldiers while inspecting the defenses of the capital.

Seventy-one runaway slaves from Maryland and Virginia were confined in Washington

Contrabands coming into Union lines. The soldiers are wearing havelocks. *Library of Congress.*

jails during the first two months following Lincoln's inauguration. Most of them had been arrested by Union soldiers stationed in the city, and some said that they thought they would be free if they could reach Washington. Sixty-four of their number had been returned to their masters, and the others were held to be returned when called for. Three slaves, caught as they came into the city from Virginia over the Anacostia Bridge and kept under guard at the Navy Yard, were reclaimed and delivered to their owner after he had proved "his property right in them, and satisfied the Colonel in charge that he was a Union man." Under the caption, "A Double Seceder," the press reported that one "run-away slave, who was set to work and made to keep at it, said: 'Golly, dis nigger neber hab tu work so hard afore; guess dis chile will secede once moah.'"

Reports of skirmishes and minor attacks between the military forces of the North and South began to make headlines. Like a lighted fuse they ran through the pages toward the explosion of declared war: "ENGAGEMENTS AT AQUIA CREEK; SKIRMISH AT FAIRFAX COURT-HOUSE; FIGHT IN WESTERN VIRGINIA; THE AFFAIR AT BIG BETHEL—captures and seizures of vessels and men." Eleven states had now seceded from the Union: South Carolina, Mississippi, Florida, Alabama, Georgia, Louisiana, Texas, Virginia, Arkansas, North Carolina, and Tennessee. Meanwhile the Confederate Congress had met in Montgomery, Alabama, and Jefferson Davis, the United States Secretary of War in the Cabinet of President Franklin Pierce, and a former Senator from Mississippi, was chosen President of the Confederate States.

Simon Cameron, Lincoln's first Secretary of War, issued orders which showed the course events were taking. He directed that female nurses, who had proper training, be employed instead of men in the general hospitals whenever possible, the nurses to be over thirty years of age, so that men would be released for duty elsewhere. An answer came from two hundred Sisters of Charity who said they were ready to enlist and take charge of hospitals, ambulances, or any post, far or near, where the cause of humanity could be served. Eventually they staffed the Lincoln Hospital (East Capitol and Fifteenth Street, Northeast) while another group, the Sisters of Mercy, served at the Stanton Hospital.

Among the most notable individuals to respond were three women from Massachusetts. One was Dorothea Dix, experienced in social work, who was appointed Superintendent of Nurses. Another was Clara Barton, prim and timid, who later organized and was the first President of the American Red Cross. The third, Louisa Alcott, known for her poetical writings, was unacquainted with blood and dirt. Groups, such as the Christian Commission at 500 H Street, Northwest, also devoted full time to looking after the needs of men in the Union Army.

Dorothea L. Dix. *National Archives.*

The U. S. Christian Commission at 500 H Street Northwest. *Library of Congress.*

Clara Barton. *National Archives.*

Louisa M. Alcott. *National Archives.*

Among exciting events in the capital during the summer of 1861 were the Army balloon experiments of Professor T. S. C. Lowe, who made a number of ascensions above the city and also over battle grounds. These photographs show the gas generating

Publications in the two capitals of the divided Republic quoted and taunted one another with any morsel of ridicule they could dig up. The Montgomery press reported: "The Cabinet of the Confederate States read President Lincoln's proclamation amid bursts of laughter." And Washington residents enjoyed the quip: "A War Horse Coming Northward—We learn that President Davis' war horse is on its way to Richmond. Accompanying the animal is the President's saddle, on the horn of which is a compass, to be used in case the rider should lose his way."

Among exciting events in the capital that summer were the army balloon experiments of twenty-nine-year-old Professor T. S. C. Lowe, who was sponsored by another professor, Joseph Henry, Director of the Smithsonian Institution. Lowe made a number of ascensions from the Columbian Armory grounds, taking with him a telegraph having a

connecting wire with the White House. From his aerial perch, claimed to have been five hundred feet, but probably not more than half that much, he sent a dispatch to President Lincoln reading:

Balloon Enterprise
Washington, D.C., June 18, 1861
To the President of the United States:
This point of observation commands an area near fifty miles in diameter. The city, with its girdle of encampments, presents a superb scene. I have the pleasure in sending you this first dispatch ever telegraphed from an aerial station, and in acknowledging indebtedness to your encouragement for the opportunity of demonstrating the availability of the science of aeronautics in the military service of the country.

T. S. C. Lowe

Since the balloon could rise to heights beyond the range of Confederate shellfire, Lowe's observations became important.

Such experiments received the approval of Lincoln and War Secretary Cameron, but not General Winfield Scott who was jokingly credited with having ascended in Lowe's balloon and discovering Jeff Davis, Confederate Generals Robert E. Lee and Pierre G. T. Beauregard, having breakfast in Virginia with eighty thousand rebel troops encamped around them. One report described Lowe's new silk balloon, inflated at the gasometer in the First Ward, as having reeled across the Aqueduct to ride above the Virginia hills and look down upon scattered camps and a high cloud of dust near Fairfax Court House. Once, rebels, trying to shoot him down, overcharged their guns and elevated them too high. When fired, the guns burst and killed the rebels. Lowe witnessed the incident and described it in his report to army officers. His activities, however, proved to Northern military authorities that the balloon could be used advantageously in ascertaining the numbers and movements of enemy troops. Within a few months "Balloon Reconnaissance" became a familiar phrase in army dispatches and developed a source of information unknown before.

Curiosity, and a spirit of adventure, led to a journalist soaring upward in Lowe's balloon and describing the event as "TAKING A RISE— Yesterday afternoon Prof. Lowe was exercising his balloon in the clouds for the benefit of those who were solicitous of an aerial trip, and were willing to pay their proportion of the gas bill. The fare was not high considering the expenses of an inflation, and all who went up, we believe, held that they fully got their money's worth. It was our good fortune to participate in one of these trips. We liked it, rather, and vote for the 'air line' above all other modes of travel. Up we slid 500 or 1,000 feet into the evening sky, with so placid a

equipment, which he invented, ready for operating near the Capitol, and Professor Lowe standing, with hand raised, beside his balloon as it is being inflated. *National Archives.*

motion that our vehicle seemed stationary and the earth sinking away from us.

"It was wonderful to see people beneath, dwarf in proportions to squat lilliputian figures, and it was odd to hear their voices 'simmer down' from the hoarse huzzah to the faintest bee-like hum. Then we began to notice the extreme beauty of the basin in which Washington lies, as seen from our elevation; not unlike the famed Paris basin as seen from the commanding points above that city. Just beneath us were the graceful sinuosities of the Smithsonian drives and walks, and Downing's admirable plan of these grounds was seen for the first time as a comprehensive whole. Then there was the checkerwork and radii of our city's system of streets all unfolded, with horses and vehicles creeping along insect-like.

"Elsewhere the stately Potomac was seen stretching far into the distance southward till attenuated to a silver thread. On the Virginia shore the white tents of the encampments stood out in minute dotted relief from the background of verdant foliage-draped hills. To the East of North could be seen bright flashes and puffs of smoke, showing where the Rhode Island boys were practising their batteries. At this time an open umbrella, dropped from the balloon, sailed down parachute fashion taking its time to reach the earth; and

J. Wells, del.

Washington and vicinity, showing points of interest, including nearby forts and battle grounds. *Library of Congress.*

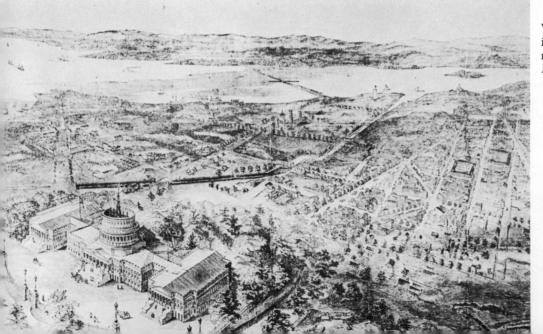

A sketch, drawn from a balloon anchored above the city, shows the Capitol in the foreground, with its unfinished dome topped by a huge crane and scaffolding. In the background, the Long Bridge (Fourteenth Street Bridge) crosses the Potomac River to Virginia. Steamboats and sailing vessels are off the Sixth and Seventh Street wharves

W. Ridgway, sc.

1. Matthias Point.	9. Manassas Junction.	17. Aqueduct Bridge.	25. Capitol.
2. Aquia Creek.	10. Bull Run.	18. Long Bridge.	26. Navy Yard.
3. Shipping Point.	11. Centreville.	19. Georgetown.	27. Arsenal.
4. Fredericsburg.	12. Fairfax Court House.	20. Washington.	28. Maryland Shore.
5. Mount Vernon.	13. Vienna.	21. President's House.	29. Fort Washington.
6. Alexandria.	14. Falls Church.	22. Smithsonian Institute.	30. Indian Head.
7. Orange & Alexandria R.R.	15. Arlington House.	23. Patent Office.	31. Maryland Point.
8. London & Hampshire R.R.	16. Chain Bridge.	24. General Post Office.	32. Port Tobacco.

33. Forts Scott, Albany, Runyon, Richardson, Craig, Woodbury, Corcoran, Bennett, &c.

farther to the left, and beyond them are the Navy Yard and Marine Barracks. To the far right is Mason's Island (Theodore Roosevelt Island) and the Aqueduct Bridge, now known as Key Bridge.

Pennsylvania Avenue extends from the rear of the Capitol to the long Treasury Building which blocks its way at Fifteenth Street, Northwest. At lower right, a train puffs along the Baltimore & Potomac Railroad tracks to the station, passing sheds used by workers for sheltering material needed in construction of the Capitol dome.

The inlet of the old City Canal, which crosses the center of the drawing, was approximately at Seventeenth Street and Constitution Avenue, Northwest. The unfinished Washington Monument is seen at the far right with the buildings of the Smithsonian Institution some distance behind it. At the extreme left is the Eastern Branch River, with the United States Arsenal and the Penitentiary located on Greenleaf's Point at its right. *National Park Service.*

soon after we made our descent in the same tranquil frame of mind. On stepping out the sensation was something like that from getting down from skates after some tall sport on the ice—terra firma seemed decidedly flat and common-place to the tread. Yes, we vote for the 'air line' and want no better conductor through the blue etherial than Prof. Lowe!"

Another professor, Dr. Francis Lieber of the Columbia College of Law, got his name into print by calling on Lincoln and presenting him with a diploma certifying that the honorary degree of LL.D. (Doctor of Law) had just been conferred upon the President by the college "in token of his devotion to those principles of freedom, law, order, and union, which should always find their representative in the Chief Magistrate of the land."

Military orders by General Beauregard at Manassas Junction in Virginia, some thirty-five miles west from Washington, and by General Winfield Scott in the capital, confined citizens of the North and South to separate territories. Thus the two armies, taking up positions on stated military boundaries, severed the last contact of Washington families with relatives and friends remaining behind Confederate lines. While brother faced brother, ready for combat with sword and gun on the field of battle, Congress met in special session to hear the Message of the President of the United States. Lincoln's words, on July 4, 1861, were a warning to all men who would suppress right with military might.

Our popular Government has often been called an experiment. Two points in it our people have already settled—the successful *establishing* and the successful *administration* of it. One still remains—the successful *maintenance* against a formidable internal attempt to overthrow it. It is now for them to demonstrate to the world that those who can fairly carry an election can also suppress a rebellion; that ballots are the rightful and peaceful successors of bullets; and that when ballots have fairly and constitutionally decided, there can be no successful appeal back to bullets; there can be no successful appeal except to ballots themselves at succeeding elections. Such will be the great lesson of peace, teaching men that what they cannot take by an election, neither can they take it by a war; teaching all the folly of being the beginners of a war.

In celebration of the national holiday, Lincoln, with General Scott, reviewed a patriotic parade which included the Garibaldi Guards, a rowdy group who tried to surpass the New York Fire Zouaves in uniforms and hilarity.

As the people in Washington read reprints from Southern newspapers in their own dailies, they realized it would be only a matter of time until the growing armies clashed head on. Late in June, the report of a Confederate war correspondent, quoted from the Louisville *Courier*, said: "The return of [General George B.] McClellan to his post, as commander of the Abolition army in Western Virginia, is deemed of sufficient significance to make all preparations for repelling an attack; and notwithstanding the profound secrecy pertaining to the movement of our troops, at Headquarters the briskness of things generally, coupled with the hasty departure of two regiments for Harper's Ferry, at two o'clock this morning, justifies me in saying that there will be 'somebody hurt' in a few days."

They did not have long to wait. By mid-July bold-faced type in the Washington press spelled out "EXTRA—EXCITING WAR NEWS— GEN. McCLELLAN'S VICTORY COMPLETE — PEGRAM'S ROUT COMPLETE—HE IS OVERTAKEN AND SURRENDERED WITH THE REMNANT OF HIS TROOPS: McClellan has now 1,000 prisoners, with all their artillery, baggage wagons, tents, etc., even to their tin cups." McClellan had won the battle of Rich Mountain in Western Virginia.

On the twenty-first of the month (Sunday), cannon spread the thunder of battle over farm lands in the neighborhood of Manassas Junction, Virginia. As the dull, heavy sound was heard in Washington, and the smoke of artillery rolled skyward, many residents jumped into conveyances or on horseback and raced over roads leading to the fighting at Bull Run. No one wanted to miss being present at the first great Union victory. "Tomorrow," they said, "we will ride on with the Union army into Richmond." By late afternoon, however, they discovered they were galloping in the wrong direction. Federal troops were retreat-

President Lincoln, General Winfield Scott, and members of the Cabinet, review a July Fourth patriotic parade which included the Garibaldi Guards. *Library of Congress.*

On the road to Bull Run, as sketched by artist Frank Beard. *Library of Congress.*

Soldiers and civilians stampede from the defeat of federal troops at the first battle of Bull Run. *Library of Congress.*

The first battle of Bull Run, July 21, 1861. *National Archives.*

ing and leaving panic in their wake. The mad scramble to get back to Washington left highways jammed with over-turned vehicles, runaway horses, all sorts of army equipment, and civilians' wearing apparel. Newspapers blamed "unmilitary teamsters and still more unmilitary sightseers" on or near the battlefield for the disaster.

"The battle wagons, by the hundred, were stationed on a hill, in view of a large body of the army engaged," read one report. "A part of our artillery was ordered to the ground occupied by these teams, and the teamsters were ordered to leave the ground as fast as possible. They took the order for an alarm, and began to drive wildly from the field. The civilians in the same neighborhood took flight along with them. The troops saw this, and a brigade, being in motion to take up a new position, mistook the movement for a flight or retreat, or converted the movement into a retreat. Then commenced the panic, and it quickly became a sea of confusion. The battle was a grand victory up to this time, and it stands as that yet, notwithstanding the retreat, for there were twenty-five thousand of our troops on the field that were not brought into action. The burden of the day, from eight

64

"Quaker guns" found in a rebel defense at nearby Centerville, Virginia, after evacuation of Manassas by Confederate troops. *National Archives.*

Wounded Zouave in a Washington hospital after the defeat at Bull Run.

in the morning till six in the evening, was borne by unrelieved troops, thousands of them without their breakfast, and all without food, except a cracker or two each."

"Quaker guns" (large tree trunks) found in some rebel defenses at nearby Centerville, Virginia, after evacuation of Manassas by Confederate troops, were first believed to have been their only "protection" in those quarters. However, later inspection proved that numerous field batteries and heavy guns had been hauled into position at such points.

But the struggle paid dividends; more men and money poured into Washington to avenge the losses sustained by the Union army. Untrained and undisciplined, the volunteers presented many problems to those entrusted with organizing and drilling them. General George B. McClellan's order, making it incumbent on Brigadier Generals to have "a division drill by trumpet" at least once a week, followed criticism that the volunteers did not know a single call "on the brazen instrument," and it was highly necessary that they be fully instructed in such military tactics.

The first Union defeat at Bull Run also made apparent the need for surrounding the capital's circuit of thirty-four miles with

65

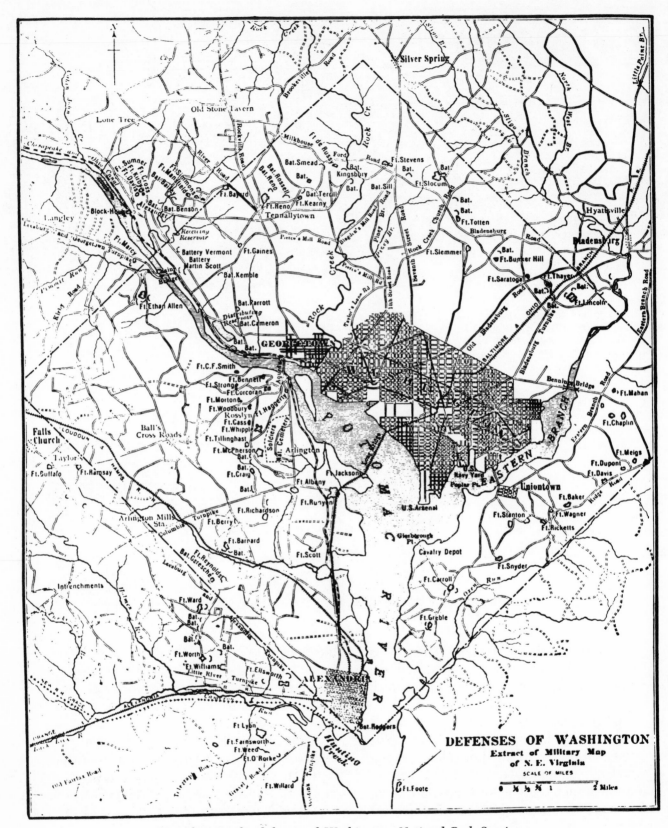

Map showing the defenses of Washington. *National Park Service.*

Old Fort Washington. *National Park Service.*

powerful fortifications. Old Fort Washington, described as an obsolete stone and brick fort built between 1814 and 1824, and located eleven miles south of the capital on the Maryland side of the Potomac, was the only protection against rebel attack when hostilities actually began. Early in 1861 a garrison of forty Marines had been sent there when it seemed war was imminent.

Now plans were drawn up and construction began on forts such as Richardson, Totten, and Bunker Hill. At the same time Fort Massachusetts (later Fort Stevens) was built on the Seventh Street Road to defend its main approach from the north. All of these were part of an elaborate chain of defenses when completed. Eventually this consisted of sixty-eight forts and batteries with emplacements for 1,120 guns on which 807 cannons and ninety-eight mortars were mounted. There

One of the defenses of Washington was Fort Massachusetts, built in August, 1861, along the Seventh Street Road (Brightwood Avenue) just north of the capital, to defend the principal approach to the city. Later the name was changed to Fort Stevens, in honor of the Union hero, Brig. Gen. Isaac B. Stevens, who fell at Chantilly, Virginia (September 1, 1862) while leading his troops against the enemy.

Grand Cavalry and Artillery review at Washington, September 24, 1861.

also were ninety-three manned batteries for field guns and twenty miles of rifle trenches connecting the main works.

Prince Jerome Napoleon of France, then visiting Washington, had dined with President Lincoln, attended reviews of the Union army, and later had inspected camps and fortifications on the right bank of the Potomac. After expressing much surprise and admiration for the rapidity with which the vast material for warfare had been collected, he made no comment on the troops but added that it would take many months to get all the Union forces ready for successful action.

Reports of battles in Missouri (Wilson's Creek), and off the coast of North Carolina (Cape Hatteras) were of little interest to people in Washington who were frightened by rumors of an approaching battle across the river from them. The press endeavored to lessen their fears by saying that "the circumstances on which they are based amount to little more than the gradual advance of the scouting outposts of Beauregard's army to points almost within range of the guns of the fortifications of the United States; which, however, have not been attempted to be held [by the enemy] so far, for more than sufficient time in which to make reconnaissance. It is by no means improbable that if the enemy perseveres in making such reconnaissance, a considerable affair of outposts may come off within, possibly, twenty-four hours, somewhere not more than four or five miles distant in a direct line from the Capital; as such collisions almost invariably grow out of such advances.

"We state this fact that our fellow-citizens

may at once know, if hearing the boom of artillery over the river, just what it amounts to Gen. McClellan [who had just been made Commander-in-chief] is constantly in the saddle, is well informed as to all the movements and plans of the enemy, and is certainly prepared for them at all points, from Harper's Ferry to Point Lookout."

With everyone clamoring for more detailed news, the United States War Department issued a General Order under the heading, "Giving Information To The Enemy." On the date it was published, one editor wrote: "It is evident that the Government has been reluctant to move against newspapers aiding and abetting the enemy (without intending to do so) by the publication of news of military operations and preparations, the promulgation of which may be incompatible with the public interest. That's to say, before having given them the warning involved in this order. Hereafter we shall probably find the Baltimore and northern press as silent concerning the movements and preparations of Union troops in their midst as the Washington papers have been of late, necessarily."

Prince Jerome Napoleon visits Washington and attends a reception in his honor at the White House. The President, Seward, and the prince are seen on the portico at upper right. The Marine Band plays for the guests on the pavilion in the background beyond which is the unfinished Washington Monument.

The county jail at the corner of Fourth and G Streets, Northwest. *Library of Congress.*

Secrets of the Prison House—the Black Hole of Washington. From sketches made on the spot by newspaper artist A. Lumlby. *Library of Congress.*

The increasing number of troops and volunteers passing through the capital on their way to the front necessitated a bigger and better police force. A bill, passed by Congress on the day of adjournment, provided for the appointment by the President, with the consent of Congress, of five commissioners, who, with the Mayors of Washington and the adjoining city of Georgetown, would serve as the Board of Police. The police force was to consist of a superintendent, ten sergeants, and such number of patrolmen as conditions required. The regular force was not to exceed one hundred and fifty men but there was to be no limit to the number employed for special purposes.

The Board of Police was to preserve the public peace, to prevent crime and arrest offenders, to protect the rights of persons and property, to guard the public health, to preserve order at elections, to remove nuisances existing in the public streets, roads, alleys, highways, and other places, and to protect strangers and travelers at steamboat and ship landings and railway stations. Members were to be known as the Metropolitan Police. Little

did they realize what was in store for them. Within a few weeks the Mayor himself was in jail.

Mayor Berret, a Democrat, had agreed to take the oath indicated in the Act of Congress by which the Board of Police was created, but he had objected to the form sent in by the Interior Department which had been administered to other members. It contained an oath of allegiance and support to the Constitution of the United States. After declining to take the oath, the Mayor submitted a written opinion of James M. Carlisle, City Attorney, to the effect that the mayors of Washington and Georgetown, being *ex officio* members of the Board of Police, were not obliged to take any oath of office to qualify them for service with the Board, and Mayor Barret said that he adhered to that opinion. But Edward Bates, United States Attorney General, also gave an opinion in writing that the oath Mayor Berret refused to take was the one required under the Act of Congress. The Board, therefore, passed a resolution by unanimous vote that he was not qualified to act as one of its members.

The old Capitol Prison at First and A Streets, Northwest, where military offenders, prisoners of state, and captured rebels were confined. *Library of Congress.*

ARRIVAL OF HORSES AT WASHINGTON FOR THE ARMY.—[Sketched by our Special Artist.]

Arrival of horses at Washington for the Federal Army. *Washington Public Library.*

The following morning (August 24) he was arrested at his residence by men of the Provost Marshal's Guard and taken to Fort Lafayette, a federal prison in New York harbor. Nothing was found in his home nor on his person to connect him with the Confederacy. The cause of his arrest never was made public but newspapers stated that it probably was on grounds other than his refusal to take the prescribed oath. The contents of letters (though never publicly revealed),

Rose O'Neal Greenhow, the "beautiful rebel of Sixteenth Street," and her daughter in the courtyard of the old Capitol prison. *Library of Congress.*

which had fallen into the hands of army officials, may have questioned his loyalty. After several weeks' imprisonment, an order from the State Department directed his release on the condition that he take the oath of allegiance to the United States against any and all enemies, and also resign the office of mayor. He lost no time complying with the request. The action taken against him warned all citizens, high and low, that nothing less than loyalty to the Union would be tolerated by the Federal Government. At the time of his arrest, Richard Wallach, who had been elected President of the Police Board, was named Mayor of Washington by a joint session of the councils of Washington and Georgetown. The usual ceremonies brought him into office: "He was serenaded and addressed the crowd."

In the lineup of those arrested was the Confederate spy, Mrs. Rose O'Neal Greenhow, the aunt of Mrs. Stephen Douglas, whose home was opposite St. John's Church on Sixteenth Street, Northwest, in view of the White House. Known to the press as the "beautiful rebel of Sixteenth Street," she openly boasted of her activities in behalf of the South. For some time her address was Capitol Hill Prison.

Meanwhile, few appointments had been made by the Police Board and the city was

still without an adequate police force. Complaints of the numerous culprits at large in Washington piled up at police headquarters and delay in bringing them to judgment brought public criticism to the newspapers. "Messrs. Editors," one resident wrote, "Reckless and rapid driving through the streets and avenues of our city have become quite common since its introduction by the military. As this is in direct violation of the law, and endangers the lives of foot passengers—men, women, and children—the Civil Authorities are appealed to, that the police be directed in all cases to arrest the offenders, in order that they may be made to pay the penalty for such violation. The attention of the Provost Marshal to this practice on the part of the military is respectfully called."

Similar reproofs turned up at intervals. "How Horses Are Spoiled At Willard's," another complained. "The Metropolitan Police will please read the following: The dismounting officers and civilians, whose *horses are to be held* while they go into Willard's for a half hour or more, are *oftenest strangers,* and quite unaware of the mischievous hands to which they commit the unfortunate animals. They require to be humanely apprised and the class of officious little rascals who rush up with the offer to hold the horse will enjoy the half hour

or more of the owner's absence in making the horse vicious, and in spoiling his hooves, by galloping up and down on the hard pavements. Everybody who has stayed at the hotel knows how the little rascals play tricks with these 'held horses' racing with them, twitching their mouths, and in every way trying the temper and feet of the poor animals. But the owners are *oftenest strangers,* we repeat, who do not know of this mischief till it is done. Common mercy to brute animals, as well as kindness to strangers, it seems to us, requires that the police officers, who are continually witnesses to this nuisance, should put a check upon it, by the very easy correction of the boys. A word of timely reproof would stop it all."

The frequent sale of condemned horses by the Government indicated the manner in which they were used by "teamers" as well as by officers and men in the saddle, another citizen related. He suggested that strict accountability be instituted and such offenders be punished, under a law in which civil magistrates had jurisdiction, for cruelty to animals. "Suppose the new policemen be on the alert, and make a few examples," he added. There also was a complaint about the "hollow flanks" of the horses and the Government's shameful neglect in feeding them.

Then came the rebellion of the horses. A large number of them broke loose at night from a government corral near the Observatory and stampeded through the streets. The clatter of their hooves on the pavements awakened many citizens before the horses could be captured; but the horses won that rebellion. The Government built larger corrals on the outskirts of the District and complaints in the press of their ill-treatment dwindled. Reckless civilian drivers were also picked up and brought to justice. Nevertheless, Washington continued to have a traffic problem.

Other complaints of police laxity in matters such as arresting persons selling or giving liquor to soldiers, kidnappers of fugitive slaves, Confederates escaping from the Old Capitol Hill Prison, and the increasing number of streetwalkers and gyp artists, also brought results. Over a period of two months, arrests totaled 2,113 persons, more than 300 of

Shelling Confederate cavalry across the Potomac River from the heights of Great Falls, by Major West, of Campbell's Pennsylvania Artillery, October 4, 1861. *National Park Service.*

whom were turned over to military authorities. Fines imposed for offenses against the United States amounted to $1,440; those under ordinances of the Corporation of Washington brought $3,288.86 to the city's treasury. "The number of arrests argues well for the activity of the police force," commented the press. With money on hand, the force went on a buying spree. New uniforms of blue pants, coats, and caps soon identified those in the service of the Metropolitan Police.

As the war advanced, national events affected the local scenes. People scanned

newspapers, gathered in groups, asked questions, most of them hoping the bloodshed would soon be over, little realizing that 2,400 combats and battles would make up the total before the end. Thus the level of morale rose and fell with each report of victory or defeat for Union troops, and nerves were often jittery if guns thundered too near the capital.

Rejoicings brought about by news of a "Brilliant Union Victory—Capture of Fort Clark and Fort Hatteras and 630 Prisoners—Prizes, Guns, and Ammunition Taken!" by General Benjamin F. Butler, were subdued

74

on the morning of September 3 when citizens again feared an invasion of the city. Evidence that their fears were unfounded appeared under a column heading, "THE FIRING TODAY: The heavy booming of cannon heard this morning created quite a buzz of excitement on the street corners and at the Center Market, from which latter place some of the old lady customers scuttled away to their respective homes with half filled baskets, and in a state of considerable trepidation. The first impression was that the firing was in the direction of Munson's Hill, and a good many glasses were at once directed in that direction, but all seemed as quiet as a summer's morning in that locality, with few Confederate soldiers visible, and those pursuing the even tenor of their way. All seemed equally tranquil at our own camps over the river with the exception of a little artillery practice by one of our companies near the Potomac, this side of Alexandria. The heavy firing, however, was evidently in the direction of the Chain Bridge, and was soon set down by those posted, as practice gunnery also. It was continued for two or three hours."

The Chain Bridge Battery located at the Maryland end of the bridge. The fire of these two 12-pounders protected the bridge and were a part of the defenses constructed there in August, 1861, soon after the first battle of Bull Run. *National Park Service.*

Burning of the E Street Infirmary on November 4, 1861, and rescue of the sick and wounded. Note fire-fighting equipment used at this time. *Library of Congress.*

In October another roar of federal artillery came from the same direction at Great Falls when Union troops shelled Confederate cavalry on the other side of the Potomac. It was believed they had stored a large quantity of provisions and supplies in a barn which was hit and emptied of rebels in short order. But that same month the pendulum swung once more from a "glorious victory" at Harper's Ferry to the Ball's Bluff disaster near Leesburg, Virginia.

Press reports of the burning of the E Street Infirmary (also known as the Washington Infirmary) between 4th and 5th Streets, Northwest, which was supervised by the Sisters of Charity, brought horror to capital residents.

During the early morning of November 4th it "was discovered to be on fire. It contained, at the time, from ninety to one hundred sick and wounded soldiers and a considerable number of other Government patients. The fire is believed to have originated in a defective flue from the furnace, which was located in the cellar under the center of the main building to the rear. The rooms of the Sisters of Charity were in this addition, over the furnace, and the medical cadets had a room above. The rooms of the Sisters were filled with smoke about half an hour after midnight. They had barely time to hurry into their clothing and escape, leaving all but the clothing they had on in the burning building.

"The Metropolitan Police were soon upon the ground and ran through the house arousing the inmates, and about this time the scene was awful in the extreme. All of the sick and wounded able to rise wrapped the bed clothing around them and escaped from the building, and the shrieks of those unable to do so were terribly piercing and thrilled the hearts of all who heard them. Some patients were carried to City Hall, some to Judiciary Square schoolhouse, some to Griffins Battery, some to Old Trinity Church on 5th Street, and many to private residences. It is believed by the officers of the institution that all the patients were rescued with the exception of one; an aged woman named Mrs. Hussey, who cannot be found and it is supposed she has perished in the flames.

"One hour and more after the fire was discovered, a single alarm bell was rung, and it was at least an hour after that before any fire engines arrived.

"By 6 o'clock this morning nothing remained of the Washington Infirmary but a mass of blackened walls and smoking timbers." The building was replaced by the Judiciary Square Hospital, often visited by Mr. Lincoln.

No opportunity for serenades and torch-light processions was overlooked by the soldiers in the capital. The promotion of General George B. McClellan in November to succeed General Winfield Scott, retired, as Commander-in-Chief of the United States Army, brought out one of the biggest demonstrations the city had witnessed since the outbreak of the war. Some two thousand men of General Louis Blenker's division, carrying lighted torches, marched to the White House where they were greeted by the President. The procession then marched around Lafayette Square, and halted in front of McClellan's residence. There General Blenker and staff were received by the new Commander-in-Chief in the presence of William H. Seward,

Torch-light procession of General Blenker's Division in honor of General McClellan, the new Commander-in-chief of the United State Army. *Library of Congress.*

Exterior and interior of the United States General Hospital at Georgetown, formerly the Union Hotel. *National Archives, Washington Public Library.*

now Secretary of State, Simon Cameron, Secretary of War, and a number of army officers. Music, speeches, and fireworks claimed the attention of the people for a brief period that evening. They applauded McClellan for his expressed determination that no power on earth, neither that of the press nor of politics, would keep him from bringing the rebellion to a speedy end with victory for the Union.

That month General McClellan held a Grand Review of Union troops at Bailey's Cross Road in Virginia. The President, accompanied by Seward and Cameron, drove the eight miles to see five thousand soldiers and their officers parade before them while thousands of Washington citizens, who also had made the journey, cheered until they were hoarse or exhausted.

With winter at hand, people became alarmed over a possible scarcity of coal and wood for household purposes. The assurance

The United States General Post Office at Seventh and F Streets, Northwest, and employees in the dead letter division. *Library of Congress, Washington Post.*

that railroad transportation now was ample to supply such needs somewhat calmed their anxiety. But the increasing habit of relieving war-torn nerves by finding something to grumble about never failed. At all hours of the day and night army wagons and artillery rumbled through the streets mingling with the clatter of galloping squads of cavalry, and long lines of oxen carted heavy guns to defenses surrounding the Capitol. "What the state of our streets will be the coming winter, when cut to pieces by the heavy army wagons, we can hardly imagine," the press predicted. The government's decision to erect a bridge for military purposes across the Potomac at Georgetown, while ignoring the city's traffic needs, also brought this complaint: "If the cry of citizens for street railways [horse cars] should awaken an earnest effort in Congress for their construction, we can cheerfully wade through one more winter of discouragement and mud." And that was exactly what they did, for a city railway was not realized until the following year when ground was broken near the Capitol and workmen began taking up the cobblestones preparatory to laying the track. The company discarded all ceremonies beyond employing a vigorous Hibernian, armed with a pick, to make the first impression in the ground before thirty laborers went to work.

It was to be known as the Washington and Georgetown Railroad, the connecting link between the two adjoining cities bound by a mutual defense during the war. Buildings in the older city also were converted to government use. One of these was the popular Union Hotel, which became the United States General Hospital, enlisting among its personnel the poetic Louisa Alcott.

Reports of Union victories gave some relief to the people of Washington as the holidays approached. The forts at Port Royal, an equal distance between Charleston and Savannah, the railroad between the two cities, the town of Beaufort, and a large quantity of supplies, had been captured. "REBELS SHELLED OUT FROM THEIR FORTIFICATIONS WITH GREAT LOSS," read the headlines. "THEY RETREAT IN A PERFECT ROUT. PANIC THROUGHOUT THE SURROUNDING COUNTRY. BEAUFORT FOUND ENTIRELY DESERTED. PLANTATIONS DESERTED, EXCEPT BY THE NEGROES. CONTRABANDS COME IN DROVES TO OUR LINES." And from Brigadier General Ulysses S. Grant had come word of a "complete victory" for his troops at the Battle of Belmont, Missouri: "The city abandoned, 130 prisoners and all of rebel artillery captured," the dispatch read.

Thanksgiving Day passed with the usual suspension of business activities. Merchants,

Greeting visitors in the White House. *National Park Service.*

government officials and employees, went from church to mid-afternoon dinners of turkey, cranberry sauce, and pumpkin pie. Mayor Richard Wallach's Proclamation was a short resumé of the situation in which the city found itself: "Whilst the present year witnesses a phase of our national affairs startling to the world," he declared, "and a crisis in our country as deplorable as it is unparalleled, which has already paralyzed one section and prostrated sister cities, the citizens of Washington should especially be not unmindful of the failure of these causes to produce like effects in the metropolis of the Union, or from whence this dispensation sprang, and, in humble acknowledgment, render thanks that, as this same year approaches its close, our city is peculiarly blessed in abundant employment for all its labor, unusual mercantile prosperity, and all that ordinarily renders a community contented and happy. . . ."

Convening of the second session of Congress and the President's Message again were subjects of conversation in homes and public places. Arguments that the national capital be removed to New York City for security reasons received a general rebuke. Receptions at the White House were drawing large crowds and the holiday season, regardless of the war, was in full swing. The National Theatre, which featured many great stars of the time, music halls and other places of amusement were well patronized. One advertised an "Equestrian Season" with Monsieur Herriman, "universally recognized as the greatest living Prestidigitateur" who vied for well-filled houses with Miss Carlotta Patti, a "celebrated Cantatrice" making her first appearance in the city. A review of her concert occupied less than half the space given to the magician.

The Board of Police Commissioners suffered more criticism at this time for failure to arrest fugitive slaves, their excuse being that it was not the duty of that office to take care of such matters. It was pointed out, however, that when one "master" applied to the police to assist him in rescuing his slave-girl, the assistance was given, and the girl was placed in jail for safe-keeping.

The old National Theatre on the same site of the present building in downtown Washington. *Smithsonian Institution.*

BURNING OF THE GOVERNMENT STABLES AT WASHINGTON, D. C. FROM A SKETCH BY OUR SPECIAL ARTIST. See page 179.

Burning of the government horse stables at Washington. *Library of Congress.*

Fires, some of which destroyed large stables and burned many horses to death, produced a serious problem for the city since there was not enough fire-fighting equipment to control them. No one could explain the origin of these disasters, the greatest having occurred at a Government corral consisting of ten sheds containing about fifteen hundred or more horses. The entire city turned out to see the fire, in which some two hundred horses perished, while others (many severely burned) escaped through the quick action of spectators who cut loose their halters. The injured animals, after reaching adjacent streets, kept

moving about, kicking and jumping and shaking their heads because of the torturing pain. Those who suffered most were shot by soldiers and civilians to put them out of their misery. Hundreds of horses surviving the fire scattered in every direction, and all night long, men and boys (white and Negro), on foot and on horseback, went about the city capturing and returning them to the neighborhood of the smoldering corral. One reporter observed that it was a miracle no one was injured or killed by the frantic animals when the fire was at its height. An adjoining building also went up in smoke and several dwellings were

War scenes at and about Washington. *Library of Congress.*

greatly damaged. That the fire did not spread more havoc probably was due to mild weather. A candle discovered between the charred beams of another government stable led to the belief that arson was the cause of these catastrophies. It was hoped that a Meigs fire plug recently installed and ready to be tested would prove that an ample supply of hose and general distribution of the Potomac water pipes would make the city independent of fire engines, but apparently it failed to do so.

On Christmas Day the press requested everyone "to remember the soldiers . . . especially those who are sick and wounded, languishing in our hospitals. . . . Any contribution of nourishment and refreshment—lemons, apples, pies, jellies, or even a dish of baked apples—will afford comfort to the invalids. We invite to this object of benevolence, on this holy day, the kindness of strangers and sojourners, as well as residents. Contributions of any kind may be deposited at the Army Aid Rooms at the Patent Office for distribution."

The year in which was born the war between the states had cast a shadow over the City of Magnificent Distances.

Sin and Smoke

A balmy New Year's Day brought crowds to the streets who spoke cheerfully of the delightful weather as a good omen for the future. The President's reception at the White House was jammed with people waiting in long lines to shake his hand. The appearance of British diplomats was considered a prophetic sign that tension between the United States and England, provoked by the Trent Affair, had lessened. A possible break in the relations of the two countries had occurred when James Mason and John Slidell, Confederate envoys to Europe, were taken from the British steamer *Trent* at sea by orders of Captain Charles Wilkes, commander of a United States naval vessel. Their release on this New Year's Day ended the fear of "more than one war at a time," as Lincoln expressed it. The Union forces now had 212 warships and merchantmen in commission.

Throughout the afternoon and evening many people went to a popular restaurant at Eleventh Street and Pennsylvania Avenue, Northwest, which had opened in 1858. The owner advertised: "Something new! Greatest discovery of the Age! OYSTERS STEAMED in the shell and thoroughly cooked (far superior to a roast) in two minutes, the fastest time on record. Call and see George W. Harvey." The discovery had been made by him while trying to find a method for supplying countless orders of that seafood to impatient patrons of Harvey's Oyster House. But there were those in Washington on that balmy day who did not feel gay nor interested in succulent discoveries. Numerous arrests and fines imposed for drunkenness and disorderly conduct were evidence that a large number

New Year's reception at the White House, 1862. The bearded man in the buckskin outfit is Seth Kinman, California woodsman and hunter, who never missed a public function at the White House if he was in Washington. *National Park Service.*

The East Room in the White House during Lincoln's administration. *National Park Service.*

of people had over-indulged in all-night celebrations.

During the first week of the New Year, Horace Greeley, owner and editor of the New York *Tribune,* gave one of a series of lectures at the Smithsonian Institution. Lincoln,

Harvey's Restaurant during the Civil War was midway between the Capitol and the White House on Pennsylvania Avenue. *From a Harvey photograph.*

Secretary of the Treasury Salmon P. Chase, and several Senators and army officers, seated on the platform, heard Greeley say that he was "not yet naturalized here, but hoped the time was not far distant when he would be able to hold discussions farther South." Many persons attending the lecture had been compelled to creep under or clamber over the couplings of a long train of freight cars blocking their way. Injuries sustained by several of them brought complaints that, not only did the Orange and Alexandria Railroad Company occupy the street-crossings with cars unloading freight for private individuals and stopping all transit, but the trains were run with the most reckless disregard of human life; and citizens remonstrating with those in charge of the operations had met with foulmouthed abuse by such employees. "It is about time the police did their duty in the matter of the car nuisance," angry residents declared. But nothing was done to remedy the situation.

News that the naval forces of the Union

Horace Greeley. *National Archives.*

The Smithsonian Institution. *Library of Congress.*

were in operations against the enemy came that January in reports from Old Point, Virginia. "THE BOTTOM FALLING OUT OF THE SECESH TUB," predicated the press. "Gen. Wool Notifies The Authorities At Norfolk To Remove All Women And Children From That City. Our Fleet Prepared To Attack It! The *Minnesota* and *Cumberland* Move To That End. A New Rebel Battery Destroyed By The Guns Of The Rip Raps! Rebels Abandon Roanoke Island. Rumor Of Abandonment Of Yorktown Also! The Rebels Hurrying Troops To Norfolk." By May, United States General John Ellis Wool was in command there.

Refugees from Virginia and other southern states, upon arrival in Washington, were required to report at headquarters and take the oath of allegiance to the Union. Their occasional sprees in celebration of the event, the difficulties of some in finding lodgings and work, and the care of those who were ill, became another problem in the over-crowded city. The flagrant sale of liquor on Sunday, or in unlicensed places, and to soldiers, resulted in spurts of activity by military authorities and such newspaper reports as "MORE WASTE OF THE RAW MATERIAL—The provost guard visited the barroom of Mr. Kernan and nine barrels of whiskey were poured upon the ground." This led to many owners of drinking places putting up large cards reading: NOTHING SOLD TO SOLDIERS, or grouping the three arms of the military services with the words NO LIQUOR SOLD TO above them. Under headings HORSES AND PISTOLS, FIGHTING ALLEY, SAVED FROM SIN, local news columns devoted much space to accounts of gambling, drunkenness, rape, robbery, and murder. Counterfeit bills ("wildcat money") of various denominations also were on the loose and in bold-face type the public was warned: WATCH OUT FOR THEM! An advertisement appearing from day to day advised: "THERE'S A BETTER TIME COMING! Victims of

Refugees leaving their home, hoping to find shelter elsewhere. *National Archives.*

88

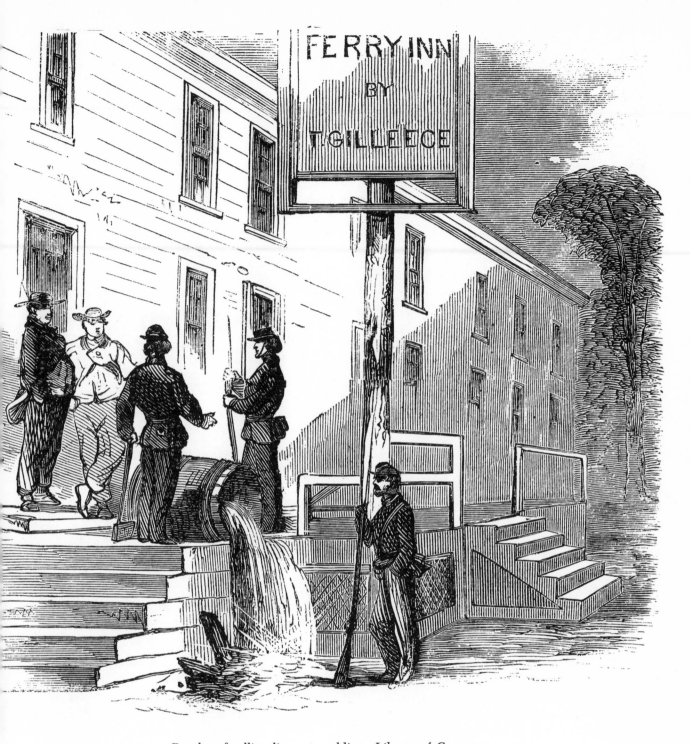

Penalty of selling liquor to soldiers. *Library of Congress.*

self abuse and secret diseases should apply at Shuman's Southern Medical House, under the Clarendens Hotel, corner Sixth Street and Pa. Avenue, immediately opposite the National Hotel, and try Dr. Southey's Celebrated London medicines. They are warranted to cure the most virulent forms of gonorrhea, gleet, syphilis, nocturnal emissions, strictures, and weakness of the bladder in from three to six days. The remedies can be sent by mail. Office hours from 9 A.M. to 10 P.M."

Surrounded by sin and smoke, the elite of

The Grand Presidential Party at the White House on February 5, 1862. *Library of Congress.*

the city gathered around gold-braided celebrities and diplomats at social functions, the most notable being given at the White House. With the enemy intermittently at the gates of the capital, the list of high-ranking Union officers included many generals and their aid-de-camps whose duties were with the army in the field. Reports of the affair caustically alluded to it as more of a victory celebration than one of ordinary significance.

The fete had the touch of Mrs. Lincoln's hand and was spoken of as the "crowning social triumph of the First Lady". She was described as elegantly dressed in white satin, with black lace flounces, a yard or more in width, festooned with white and black ribbon. She wore pearl ornaments, and a handsome

Parisian headdress with bunches of crêpe myrtle, and she carried a bouquet to match.

Maillard, the famous caterer of New York, was there with his force of trained waiters, cooks, and confectionery artists, and tables were loaded with the products of their skill. These included sweetened replicas of a temple surrounded by the Goddess of Liberty, Chinese pagodas, cornucopias, fountains with sprays of spun sugar and encircled by stars, and the American frigate *Union* with guns, sails, flags, smoke stack and all, complete in sugar, the whole supported by Stars-and-Stripes-draped cherubs. Fort Pickens also loomed up in sugar on a side table, surrounded by something more edible than barbette guns, in the shape of deliciously prepared "chicken

Mrs. McClellan.   Mrs. Lincoln.   Mrs. Senator Crittenden.

SOME OF THE PRINCIPAL COSTUMES WORN AT THE GRAND PRESIDENTIAL PARTY AT THE WHITE HOUSE, WEDNESDAY EVENING, FEBRUARY 5.

THE PRESIDENTIAL PARTY.

(Continued from page 210.)

... to the Presidential party. Early in the ... windows of the White House were brilliant ... lighted by half-past nine the entrance was thronged

with guests from a long line of carriages reaching to the avenue. The cards of invitation were received at the door, and the guests passed to the second story of the mansion, which had been thrown open for dressing-rooms. Thence they returned to the grand entrance, and were shown into the Blue Room, whence they passed to the grand saloon, or

East Room, where they were received by Mr. and Mrs. Lincoln, with a gracious welcome and a kind word. Meanwhile the marine band "discoursed sweet music" from a side room. The saloon, when filled, presented the aspect no doubt contemplated and designed by Mrs. Lincoln, of a large select and elegant private party, with its animated conver-

SOME OF THE PRINCIPAL COSTUMES WORN AT THE GRAND PRESIDENTIAL PARTY AT THE WHITE HOUSE, WEDNESDAY EVENING, FEBRUARY 5.

Dresses worn by Mrs. Lincoln and other prominent women at the Presidential party.
Washington Evening Star.

91

fixin's." There were patties topped by birds, sitting on their nests, beehives loaded with Charlotte Russe, instead of honey, and a superb *pâté de foi gras* for gourmets.

These, and other tasty morsels, were spread about in such profusion that the joint attack of the thousand or more guests failed to deplete the array. Champagne and other costly wines and liquors flowed freely. An immense Japanese punch bowl, flanked by sandwiches, biscuits, cheese, etc., contained some twenty bottles of champagne with arrack and rum in proportions to furnish a substantial foundation.

The Marine Band, under the direction of Professor Scala, played two of his musical compositions, "The President's March," and "Mrs. Lincoln's Polka." But there was no dancing for "The President and Mrs. Lincoln seemed to think that, though there may be 'a time for dancing,' this period of the national tribulation is not *the time*." It was 3 A.M. when the last guests departed, and Lincoln crawled into his big bed long enough to accommodate his height.

Lincoln's seven-foot bed in his room at the White House. *National Park Service.*

On the President's fifty-third birthday newspapers announced, "THE GREATEST UNION ACHIEVEMENT OF THE WAR. The Burnside Expedition Kill Or Capture Wise's Whole Army On Roanoke Island, Except Fifty, Who Manage To Escape! Two Thousand Rebels Taken Prisoner! One Thousand Rebels Killed And Wounded! Loss Of Union Troops Three Hundred Killed And Wounded. The Whole Rebel Fleet Captured Or Destroyed. Henry A. Wise *Non Est* At The Battle. O. Jennings Wise Shot Through The Hip, And A Prisoner. Elizabeth City Burned To The Ground. Great Consternation At Norfolk And Richmond. So Much For The Result In That Quarter Of Gen. McClellan's Strategy! ! !"

Within a week came other good news from Grant: "FORT DONELSON POSITIVELY TAKEN. 15,000 Prisoners Taken. All The Small Arms, Armaments Of The Forts, etc., Taken. Floyd Managed To Creep Off In Time To Save His Bacon. Gens. A. Sidney Johnson and Buckner Are Prisoners Of War. The Rebels Say That DuPont's Fleet And Sherman's Army Have Taken Savannah." The people in Washington also read that Bowling Green had fallen, the enemy forced to flee, and that the Stars and Stripes were floating over it. As days passed, more bold-face type brought excitement to a high pitch: "MISSOURI CLEARED OF REBELS IN ARMS. Commodore Foote's Official Dispatch Announces The Surrender Of Clarksville. More Glad Tidings From Tennessee, The People Disgusted With Secession. Gen. A. Sidney Johnson Has Offered To Surrender Nashville On Condition That Private Property Be Spared." Contradictions, coming in quick succession, had little effect upon the senses. Four days after the report that Savannah had been taken, came the news, "REBELS ADMIT SAVANNAH MUST SURRENDER WITHIN A WEEK," and on the next day, "FROM FORTRESS MONROE —Surrender Of Savannah To The Combined Fleet And Army Of The United States Confirmed." Within a week Savannah had been taken, not taken, taken—and was yet to be a Union prize.

Such conflicting reports should have warned the people that the road to victory was to be a long road. But the people wanted an end to the war, and the exciting news brought on a hysteria for its conclusion. "THE TERMS TO BE GRANTED: Everybody is inquiring, on what terms will the military operations against the insurrection be terminated," declared one newspaper, as if the fighting had already ceased. Then it went on to dictate the terms: "A hearty return to their allegiance on the part of all the people of the States in arms against the Union, except the leaders and most active supporters of the rebellion, and especially those of them who have been in the civil, military or naval service of the United States, the chief traitors and conspirators who have worked the mischief in the South. The loyalists everywhere will never be content unless they banish themselves or are duly punished in their persons, if caught."

When it was discovered that some reports were unfounded, and the war was not at an end, reaction set in, and one editor wrote: "HOWLING, OF COURSE. Some of the New York City Republican papers are already yelping at a great rate over the order of the War Department forbidding the publication of information of military movements that may by any chance aid the enemy in resisting the arms of the United States.

"Now, we venture to affirm that there is not a man of sense and information in the country not involved in a greater or less degree in the conspiracy to have the war waged to the end, of entirely abolishing the Constitution of the United States, and substituting instead a naked philo-negro despotism, who does not heartily approve the order in question. All know that indiscreet publication of Union military movements have operated on many occasions most disastrously upon the realization of the Government's military plans, while all surely realize that the restriction is to continue no longer than a pressing necessity, for its existence may rest upon those charged with the conduct of the war.

"Experience having proved that if any latitude whatever be granted to the press under a state of circumstances such as now exists, it will surely be either wantonly or ignorantly abused by more or less sensational newspaper men. It is certainly incumbent on the Govern-

Mrs. Lincoln in mourning following the death of her son Willie. *National Park Service.*

ment to guard against that contingency of license to any, if they would rigidly exclude the enemy from obtaining premature information of the current movements and aims of the different Union armies. We believe that a few short weeks will bring the war to a close if the enemy be not enabled to checkmate the movements of our several armies by and through sensational newspaper publications of facts that the public interest requires to be kept secret, if possible, for the time being."

Meanwhile, the President and Mrs. Lincoln watched over their two youngest sons ill with fever. The death of William Wallace Lincoln, their third son, on February 20, 1862, at the age of twelve years, plagued the White House for many months. Mrs. Lincoln refused to wear anything but black and was influenced by a spiritual medium named Colchester who pretended to be the illegitimate son of an English duke. Introduced to him by a seamstress in the White House, she listened at The Soldiers' Home, the summer residence of the President's family, to messages received by taps and scratches on the walls and furniture of a darkened room.

93

Some of the officers and crew on deck of the original *Monitor*. Commander John L. Worden, in straw hat, is still wearing dark glasses after being blinded in the battle with the *Merrimac*. President Lincoln visited him on this ironclad vessel. *National Archives*.

It had been customary for the Marine Band to give weekly concerts on the grounds south of the White House during the summer, but following the death of Willie she ordered an end to such entertainment. That the public in general was deprived of enjoying the concerts that entire summer because of her personal sorrow infuriated many people and Lincoln was asked to do something about it. But not until the following summer were the concerts resumed.

Still expecting an early end to the war, Washington hopefuls were rejuvenated by an official report received by Gideon Welles,

Secretary of the United States Navy, which appeared in all the newspapers. It described how the Ericsson iron-clad gunboat *Monitor* had arrived at Fortress Monroe on the night of March 8, and early the next morning was attacked by the rebel vessels, the heavy armored *Merrimac*, the *Jamestown*, and the *Yorktown*. The *Monitor* had gone to the protection of the United States *Minnesota*, lying aground just below Newport News, when it was fired upon, and likewise blasted the enemy until the two wooden vessels retired. Then the other two iron-clad vessels had continued the fight, part of the time touching each other during a four-hour siege after which the *Merrimac* retired, leaving the *Monitor* undamaged and ready to renew the battle at any moment.

Captured rebel flags on view at the House of Representatives and news of Grant's victory on the bloody field of Shiloh at Pittsburg Landing in Tennessee brought more excitement to the capital. For two days the slaughter had continued with heavy losses on each side. "The rebels fled only after Gen. A. Sidney Johnson was killed and Beauregard badly wounded," reported the press, describing the battle as "one of the bloodiest battles of modern times." It had been a close victory for Grant but the result, said the press, "is regarded there as involving the entire destruction of Beauregard's plan of the campaign in the Southwest; with the over-whelming defeat

Captured rebel flags on view in the House of Representatives, March 1862. *Washington Public Library*.

of the rebels at Island No. 10, it must amount to practical crushing out of the rebellion in that quarter."

Immediately, newly appointed Secretary of War Edwin M. Stanton issued an "Order Giving Thanks For The Recent Great Victories Over Rebels and Traitors. Ordered—
"1st. That at Meridian of the Sunday next after the receipt of this order, at the head of every regiment in the armies of the United States, there shall be offered by its Chaplain a prayer, giving thanks to the Lord of Hosts for the recent manifestation of His power in the overthrow of rebels and traitors, and invoking the continuance of His aid in delivering this nation by the arms of patriot soldiers from the horrors of treason, rebellion and civil war.
"2d. That the thanks and congratulations of the War Department are tendered to Major General Halleck for the signal ability and success that have distinguished all the military operations of his department, and for the spirit and courage manifested by the Army under his command, under every hardship, and against every odds, in attacking, pursuing and destroying the enemy wherever he could be found.
"3d. That the thanks of the Department are also given to Generals Curtis and Sigel, and the officers and soldiers of their command for matchless gallantry at the bloody battle of Pea Ridge, and to Major Generals Grant and Buell and their forces, for the glorious repulse of Beauregard at Pittsburg in Tennessee; and to Major General Pope and his officers and soldiers for the bravery and skill displayed in their operations against the rebels and traitors entrenched at Island No. 10 on the Mississippi River. The daring achievements, diligent prosecution, persistent valor and military result of these achievements are unsurpassed.
"4th. That there shall this day be a salute of one hundred guns from the United States Arsenal at Washington, in honor of these great victories."

While the cannons boomed, the people in Washington knew they had much to be thankful for on that date.

Drawing of the First Baptist Church, Washington, D. C., which John T. Ford purchased and converted into the original Ford Theatre which burned on December 30, 1862. *National Park Service.*

Ford's Atheneum, as it then was known, had been in construction for some time on Tenth Street, Northwest, just above Pennsylvania Avenue. Formerly the First Baptist Church of Washington, built in 1833, it had been purchased by John T. Ford and converted into a theatre at the cost of some $18,000. It opened on March 19 with the talented and beautiful Lucille Western in *The French Spy.* The handsome and spacious structure was well lighted, well ventilated, and elegantly furnished. It had all the assets of a successful enterprise, but it was destined to be one of several misfortunes in Ford's theatrical ventures.

April 16 witnessed a great historic event when Lincoln signed the Act abolishing slavery in the District of Columbia. It stated that all persons held to service or labor by reason of African descent were discharged and freed, and that neither slavery nor involuntary servitude, except for crime, was to exist there. Lincoln, in his Message to Congress relating to the Act, said:

"I have never doubted the constitutional authority of Congress to abolish slavery in the District, and I have ever desired to see the National Capital freed from the institution in some satisfactory way. Hence there has never been, in my mind, any question upon the subject, except the one of expediency, arising in view of all the circumstances. If there be

W. D. (Douglas) Wallach, editor and owner of the *Washington Evening Star*. Photo courtesy of *Washington Evening Star*.

matters within and above this Act which might have taken a course or shape more satisfactory to my judgment, I do not attempt to specify them. I am gratified that the two principles of compensation and colonization are both recognized and practically applied in the Act.

"In the matter of compensation, it is provided that claims may be presented within ninety days from the passage of the Act, but not thereafter, and there is no saving for minors, femes covert, insane, or absent persons. I presume this is an omission by mere oversight, and I recommend that it be supplied by an amendatory or supplemental Act."

The following month newspapers began listing the petitions filed with the Emancipation Commissioners for the purpose of estimating the money value to be placed upon slaves about to gain their freedom.

In June the election of a mayor ushered in another hectic day for Washington. James F. Haliday, a Union Democrat opposed to war and the administration, and incumbent Richard Wallach, of the Unconditional Union Party, whose brother, Douglas, owned the *Star,* were the candidates. A general idea of what occurred was revealed by that newspaper. A man named Dingle voted, and handed his vote to a commissioner as he was

leaving. The commissioner, finding the ticket unusually thick, called him back and said there was something else in it..Dingle tore it in half, threw it down, and refused to vote at all. The pieces, quickly picked up and examined, were found to be composed of two "Haliday tickets" lightly pasted together at the end so that they could be detached on dropping them into the ballot box. Knowing that the "jig was up," Dingle started to run. Several men shouted at him to come back, "but he left in two-forty time."

An Irishwoman went to the home of a neighbor who supported the Union ticket and had voted for Wallach. She took off all her clothing, got down on her knees, and prayed that her neighbor's children would be born blind, that purgatory would hold him fast when he died, and that many other evils would befall him. Finally, from sheer exhaustion, she ended her prayers and went home to bed. The neighbor rushed out for a policeman and had her arrested. Not able to give security to keep the peace, she was put in jail. Her brother then threatened to kill any Irishman in the neighborhood who had voted for Wallach, and he too was locked up. Wallach, however, won the election.

Following this local skirmish came news of the Seven Days' Battle in Virginia. "FEARFUL SLAUGHTER," read the headlines above a report that the Army of the Potomac under command of General McClellan had taken its final position on the James River where it had the co-operation of gunboats. That the army had been on the verge of defeat was evident by the dispatches: "To march or retreat or whatever else you choose to call it," one read, "is regarded here as remarkably successful and the present position of the army is entirely safe from rebel attack. We have about five hundred secesh prisoners in the guardhouse, which means an open field surrounded by guards. They are as villainous-appearing vagabonds as one would be likely to behold in a lifetime." There was no cheering as the wounded arrived at Carver Barracks, Harwood, Armory Square, and other hospitals in Washington. and a call went out for 300,000 more men.

Carver Barracks and Hospital, near Boundry (now Florida Street) between Thirteenth and Fourteenth Streets, Northwest. *Library of Congress.*

Interior of a hospital car used by Union troops to bring their sick and wounded into Washington. *Library of Congress.*

Armory Square Hospital, Sixth Street, Northwest, south of the old City Canal. *Library of Congress.*

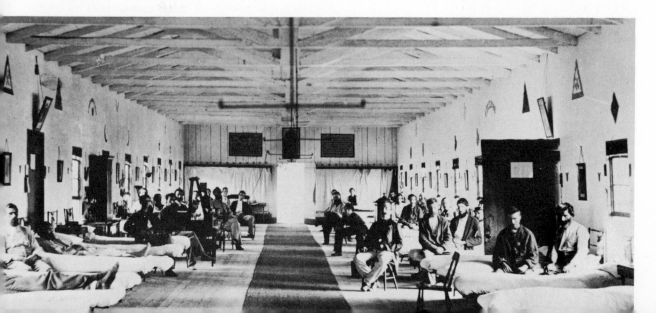

Previously, one newspaper had published a telegram received at the War Department "from an officer of high rank and character in Gen. McClellan's army." During that week of battle he had written: "The newspaper reporters having all skedaddled to prevent the people of the country being frightened to death, I will simply state that at 12 m. today [July 4] a National salute of thirty four guns was fired at the headquarters of each army corps and all the bands are playing the National airs. The men are in first-rate spirits and the General is just starting to visit all the troops. The newspaper reporters and others who have gone to the rear don't represent the Army of the Potomac. We can't be beaten, and what is more, we won't be beaten. We are all right, and always have been. If they will send re-inforcements enough to fill up our losses of sick, killed and wounded, we will take Richmond from this point. Don't believe any stampede reports you hear, there is no truth in them. Secesh is smashed up, and as soon as we can get rested and get supplies and a few more men we can use them up completely. This is a glorious Fourth of July for us—all right. We hear nothing of Secesh today. Don't fear for the Army of the Potomac. In conclusion I would just state that the Provost Marshal General found it unnecessary to order reporters to the rear, they having all skedaddled of their own accord."

A cynical note by an editor added: "We feel at liberty to say that General McClellan is grateful for the promptness with which he is being reinforced.... No comments of our own are necessary to impress upon the public mind that our army upon the Peninsula is in as fine heart as ever before...."

Few people in Washington were aware of the President's visit to McClellan. They had met at James River off Harrison's Landing where Lincoln disembarked, and rode on horseback to McClellan's headquarters. From there he went to review the army, then "dismounted and ascended the ramparts in view of the rebel pickets." No word of his whereabouts leaked through the Washington press until he had safely returned to the capital, and one reporter wrote: "We have refrained from mentioning the fact of the President's recent visit to the Army of the Potomac until this afternoon (it having been made public through yesterday's New York papers), only because deeming it prudent so to do. The country will thank him for the promptness with which he repaired to the Peninsula on this occasion, to examine for himself into the condition of the Army of the Potomac, its necessities, prospects, etc. His presence in its midst has had the happiest conceivable effect upon it; for, men and officers, high and low, all its components have implicit confidence in his patriotism and sagacity. They know he looks upon them all as the special objects of his guardianship, and seeks out to give triumph to their arms and to ameliorate the hardships and dangers to their patriotic effort in their country's behalf."

By mid-July the horse-drawn Washington and Georgetown Railroad had been completed from the Capitol to Willard's Hotel. Two passenger cars had just arrived at the depot and were transferred to the tracks for a trial run, "one being a regular passenger and the other a large open summer or excursion car. They were built in Philadelphia by Messrs. Murphy and Allison, and are very creditable pieces of workmanship. The regular car measures inside about seven by fifteen

At this time the Washington & Georgetown R.R. operated only between the Capitol and Willard's Hotel at Fourteenth Street, Northwest. *National Archives.*

98

feet, and will seat comfortably about twenty persons. The seats on the side are covered with fine silk velvet and the windows, which are of stained and plain glass combined, are furnished with cherry sash and poplar blinds, beside handsome damask curtains. The top of the car is rounded, permitting persons to stand upright without inconvenience, and rods to which loops are attached, are run from end to end. The lamp, which is surrounded by red glass, is hung up in the center in such manner as to show outside as well as in. The excursion car has seats running crosswise, and will seat twenty four persons. The car is handsomely painted, both inside and out, the prevailing color being white, while the outside is in cream color and white, with a fine painting in the center, and the words 'Washington and Georgetown R. R.' at the bottom. The wheels are of different colors, contrasting well with the body of the car, and giving it a picturesque appearance. Messrs. Murphy and Allison are making most of the cars, but others are being built by other makers, in order to have a full supply to put on as soon as the entire road is opened.

"The companies are pushing the work forward with vigor, and will have the lines from the Capitol to Georgetown stocked before the sixty days allowed by law have expired. We learn that as soon as the track can be cleared cars will commence running between the Capitol and Willard's. The cars were put on the track last night, and at 11 o'clock run up as far as Willard's, having on board a number of gentlemen cheering loudly as they passed up and being greeted with cheers from the few persons on the street at that hour."

A later report stated that the track was found to be in perfect order, "solid, smooth and substantial," and that a trial run had been made for Members of Congress, who were about to adjourn and could not be present at the formal opening of the road. By the end of the month the track had been completed from the Capitol to the State Department building and the people of Washington and Georgetown were given a free ride in the new cars. "Farewell old bus, you're nigh played out," wrote one reporter.

REVENGE.

Jones. "Do you know, Sir, what I'll do, if the Government persists in carrying out this exorbitant tax on liquors and cigars? I'll not drink another glass of liquor or smoke another cigar. No, Sir, not one!"

Revenge. *Library of Congress.*

With the railway half completed, certain citizens now complained of other matters. "The new tax upon whisky is three cents per gallon," one grumbled. "Some people think it oppressive to impose such burdens upon the necessaries of life." An additional tax on tobacco was also condemned as being exorbitant.

Prior to adjournment, Congress passed the Confiscation Act (July 17) "to suppress treason and rebellion, to seize and confiscate the property of rebels, and for other purposes." The "property of rebels" included slaves. Again Lincoln expressed his opinion on what to do with the Negro. "The Government, so far as there can be ownership, thus owns the forfeited slaves," he declared, "and the question for Congress in regard to them is, 'shall they be made free or be sold to new masters?' I perceive no objection to Congress deciding in advance that they shall be free."

Many District residents expressed their opinions too. "The sudden elevation of the Negro just emancipated," one said in print, "to an equality with white men in the Capital of the Nation is regarded as something worse than an indiscretion or an error in judgment."

At what was termed "The Great War Meeting," on the east steps of the Capitol, a disturbance occurred during a ceremony at which Lincoln, several Cabinet members, and District authorities, were present. A woman in the audience, hearing one of the speakers suggest putting the Negro on an equality with the white man, cried out "Shoot him! Shoot him!" The Provost Guard hustled her off for examination. Newspapers noted that more persons were volunteering to take the oath of allegiance to the Union because of recent arrests of "offensive disloyalists," and reports that the Government "was about to test the patriotism of our citizens."

Belle Boyd, a rebel spy, had just been brought to Washington in the custody of an officer who had arrested her in Virginia. From the train, she had been taken immediately to the Secretary of War, and after "a short audience with him," she had been hustled to the Old Capitol Prison where she was given "comfortable quarters for a season, with a soldier guarding her room." It was reported that she took her arrest as a matter of course, and was as smart, plucky, and absurd as ever.

A short time before, an article appearing in a Washington newspaper had doubtless led to her arrest. It was headed, "BELLE BOYD, NOTORIOUS IN REGION OF FRONT ROYAL, VA.," and said, "Her acknowledged superiority for machination and intrigue has given her the

Belle Boyd, rebel spy. Address: Old Capitol Prison. *National Archives.*

leadership and control of the female spies in the Valley of Virginia. She is a resident of Martinsburg when at home, and has a pious, good old mother who regrets, as much as any one can, the violent and eccentric course of her daughter since this rebellion has broken out." She was described as a sharp-featured, black-eyed woman of twenty-five, who wore a revolver in her belt and was courted and flattered by every captain and lieutenant in the service, and practiced her arts upon them at every opportunity. "During the past campaigns in the valley," the article continued, "this woman has been of immense service to the enemy. She will be now, if she can. She, therefore, should at once be passed beyond our lines, sent to Richmond, and allowed to remain with those with whom she deeply sympathises." But it was some time before she was sent to Richmond: meanwhile she was in the Old Capitol Prison, a short distance from the Great War Meeting, and must have heard the salute of thirty-four guns, and the bells of the city ringing, in celebration of that event.

The great war meeting on the east steps of the Capitol. *Washington Public Library.*

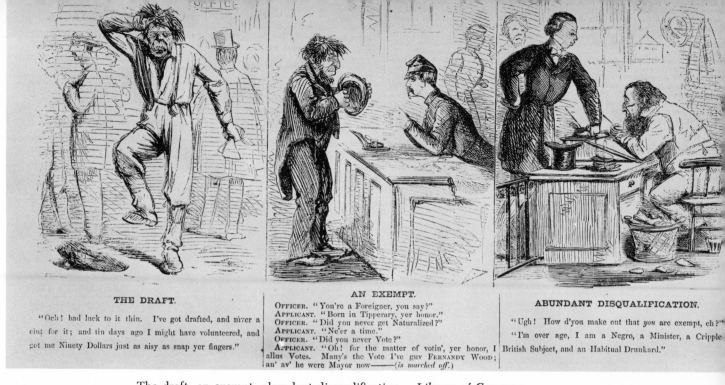

THE DRAFT.

"Och! bad luck to it thin. I've got drafted, and niver a cin; for it; and tin days ago I might have volunteered, and got me Ninety Dollars just as aisy as snap yer fingers."

AN EXEMPT.

OFFICER. "You're a Foreigner, you say?"
APPLICANT. "Born in Tipperary, yer honor."
OFFICER. "Did you never get Naturalized?"
APPLICANT. "Ne'er a time."
OFFICER. "Did you never Vote?"
APPLICANT. "Oh! for the matter of votin', yer honor, I allus Votes. Many's the Vote I've guv FERNANDY WOOD; an' av' he were Mayor now———(is marched off.)

ABUNDANT DISQUALIFICATION.

"Ugh! How d'you make out that you are exempt, ch?"
"I'm over age, I am a Negro, a Minister, a Cripple British Subject, and an Habitual Drunkard."

The draft—an exempt—abundant disqualification—. *Library of Congress.*

Rewards for the apprehension and delivery of runaway slaves increased, the sums offered being $50, $100, and $200. Entire Negro families were breaking away from masters they had served so long. Some slaves had set fire to their masters' quarters before escaping, while others were arrested and accused of assault with intent to kill. A number of female "contrabands" who were being held in the Old Capitol Prison were sent to hospitals to work as washerwomen.

Rumors of the military draft to be made in the District resulted in other flights from certain parts of the city (such as Swampoodle) by men, mostly of foreign birth, who were attempting to escape service in the Union army. The press stated that many had "packed up their duds and left—the cars taking off some two hundred fifty bound North in one day." Efforts were being made to organize a brigade for the defense of Washington among employees of the Government, and it was expected that two thousand clerks would be enrolled for that purpose.

A Negro family coming into Union lines. *National Archives.*

Oxen hauling a 15-inch Rodman gun (25 tons) through the streets of Washington. *National Park Service.*

Guns, large and small, were hauled through the streets to defenses surrounding the capital. The sixty-eight forts had mounted 905 guns and mortars, the two fifteen-inch guns at Fort Foote (Maryland), and one at Battery Rodgers (Alexandria, Virginia), being the largest. Every time one boomed, the fear of a rebel invasion excited the city. When Lincoln inspected the forts and troops from Chain Bridge to the south of the Potomac that August, a newspaper reported, "The firing heard across the river today, which occasioned some inquiry, was from the salute to the President on his round in review."

A gala serenade greeted General Michael Corcoran upon his return to Washington after being released from a Confederate prison. Early in the evening people began to gather outside Willard's and by eight o'clock the crowd in the Avenue fronting the hotel was estimated at ten thousand. The new horse-drawn cars, which continued running, had great difficulty in getting through. A number of enterprising men and boys obtained positions in the trees, but they were quickly brought down by the soldiers and the police. One man, when compelled to come down,

"leaped squarely on a canopy of heads." Every window of the hotel overlooking the celebration was filled with women, military officers, and distinguished civilians. The Speaker's Balcony blazed with gas lights, the jet of flame arranged to form the word UNION. Immediately in front of the balcony was the New York 69th—Corcoran's old regiment.

On August 30, the sound of cannons heard in Washington signaled the Second Battle of Bull Run. Union soldiers, under General John Pope, according to reports, were making "mince meat" of rebel forces and driving the enemy from the field in full retreat toward the mountains. Again, hundreds of people tried to reach the battlefield, but on the way they found federal troops stampeding toward Washington so they turned to join them. The second defeat of the Union army at Bull Run was sprinkling fresh blood upon an old battlefield. Once more the Confederate army was in control of Eastern Virginia. Once more the Union army was stunned and beaten. Once more there was a call for men—500,000 this time. Once more defeat was a spur to action and a determination to win the war.

The "situation in reverse" was humorously

Defeat of the army of General John Pope at Manassas on the Old Bull Run battle-ground. A sketch by R. Waud. *Library of Congress.*

All that was left of the Orange & Alexandria Railroad engine "Commodore" after General Pope's retreat from the second battle of Bull Run. *National Archives.*

Union soldiers examine passes at the Georgetown Ferry. *National Park Service.*

related by one newspaper under the heading, "Rather Fast." An Irishman was arrested for offering a Confederate note to a stranger. He stated that he thought Washington had been taken by the rebels, and that the bill was as good as gold. If it were worthless at the moment, he declared, it would be valuable in a few minutes, when General Stonewall Jackson arrived. The Provost Marshal's office sent him to the Old Capitol Prison where he could be among other friends of the Confederacy.

Newspaper notices of restrictions on citizens began to fill more space than the print in a prayerbook. No passes were allowed for travel to nearby encampments; permits were required by persons crossing the bridges and ferries, and for huckster wagons going to camps on the other side of the river. Women were given particular attention. It had been discovered that some were wearing "tin falsies" containing contraband liquor (Sneaky Pete and Blackberry Wine) intended for sale in the District. Military guards, stationed at such points to control the traffic became adept

at "tone testing" the females. If a flick of the finger against the breast went "ping" the falsies were removed and the contents emptied. Questions about these activities generally brought the same answer: There was a shortage of liquor in the District and anyone knew that the best liquor was made in the South.

At least a part of this was true. The Military Governor of the District had recently ordered all drinking places in the District closed "to meet the emergency of the present excited state of our population, already worked up to a high pitch by the recent battles, without the addition of liquid stimulus. As soon as the city cools down again," he added, "the restrictions will be removed, it not being the purpose of General Wadsworth to interfere further with our citizens than may be absolutely necessary in the military exigencies by which we are surrounded." But the order had little effect on gamblers, drunks, strumpets, and other notorious characters roaming the streets and cavorting in public places.

104

"Many of those who ply their vocation of entrapping foolish young men on the streets and escorting them to the vilest dens of infamy, are pointed out as the late 'pretty waiter girls' of this or that large beer or concert saloon," a reporter observed. "Others are girls who have for some time been missed from the streets, but who in anticipation of the rich harvests to be obtained from the crowds now in the city, have come forth from their dens and cellars. These characters fasten on to every soldier or other person who is at all susceptible and stick with the tenacity of leeches until they convey them to their haunts of iniquity. The morals and the good health of the community and the army require that these characters should be arrested. Quinine may be the need of the Confederate army, but copovia [copaiva, a balsam used medicinally] is certainly the necessity of ours." Some of these prostitutes were rebels who publicly praised the Confederacy and its leaders. Even-

This old print is captioned: "A Washington Gambling Hell." *Washington Evening Star.*

"Gamblers, thieves, and vagabonds—a scene in Washington," is the caption on this drawing showing a Union soldier going in the wrong direction. *Library of Congress.*

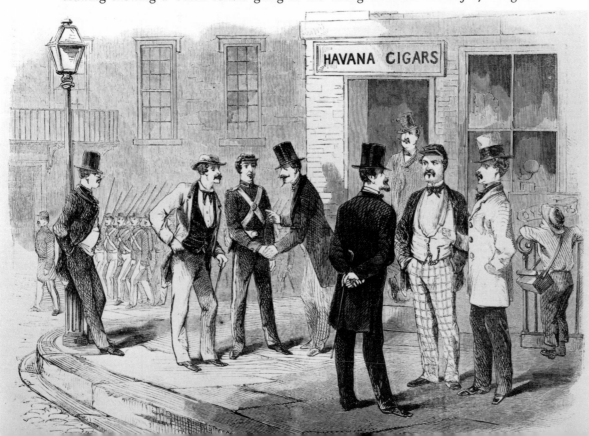

tually a large number of them were loaded onto a boat, with other "secesh" females and little baggages bound for Richmond. "It is better to give than to receive," wrote a roguish reporter.

In the midst of such excitement, the City Council went about its business in the usual way. A bill was introduced to provide for lighting the city with gas throughout the entire year from twilight to daybreak, the cost of erecting and lighting the lamps to be paid out of ward funds. It was referred. Another bill provided that no business licenses should be issued unless the applicant took the oath of allegiance to the Union. It was passed. And Washington residents were relieved by the announcement that the President had restored General George B. McClellan to command the Army of the Potomac defending the capital and the fortifications around it. Soon McClellan and his army were again in action.

Following the news that the Confederates had taken Harper's Ferry came the report of the fighting near Sharpsburg, Pennsylvania, where the two armies had faced each other across Antietam Creek until the rebels, under Lee, almost surrounded, and out of ammunition as well as provisions, retired to Virginia. "We may safely claim a complete victory," McClellan boasted in his dispatch to Major General Halleck in Washington. But his failure to pursue the rebels brought much criticism upon McClellan and his replacement at a later date.

In celebration of the preliminary Emancipation Proclamation (issued September 22, 1862), Lincoln was serenaded by a band as many people gathered at the White House. After loud calls for the President, he appeared, accompanied by John Hay, his private secretary, and addressed them. One newspaper graphically reported the speech:

"Fellow citizens—I appear before you to do little more than acknowledge the courtesy you pay me, and to thank you for it. I have not been distinctly informed why it is that on this occasion you appear to do me this honor. I suppose (An interruption. 'It is because of the Proclamation!' Cries of 'good' and applause.) I was about to say, I suppose I

"Secesh" women leaving Washington for Richmond. *Library of Congress.*

understand it. (Laughter and voices, 'That you do. You thoroughly understand it.')

"What I did, I did after very full deliberation and under a very heavy and solemn sense of responsibility. (Cries of 'good', 'God bless you,' and applause.) I can only trust in God that I have made no mistake. (Cries of 'No—all right', 'You've made no mistake yet', 'Go ahead', 'You're all right'.) I shall make no attempt on this occasion to sustain what I have done or said by any argument. (Voices, 'That's unnecessary', 'We understand it'.) It's now for the country and world to' pass judgment on it, and maybe take action upon it.

"I will say no more upon this subject. In my position I am environed with difficulties. (A voice, 'That's so'.) Yet they are scarcely so great as the difficulties of those who, upon the battlefield, are endeavoring to purchase with their blood and lives the future happiness and prosperity of this country. (Applause, long continued.) Let us never forget them. On the 14th and 17th days of this present month there have been battles bravely, skillfully, and successfully fought. (Applause.) We do not know the particulars. Let us be sure that, in giving praise to particular individuals, we do no injustice to others. I only ask you, at the conclusion of these remarks, to give three hearty cheers to all good

Lincoln and his "Emancipation Cabinet," painted by Frank B. Carpenter to whom he said, when it was suggested: "Do you think, Mr. C., that you can make a handsome picture of *me?*" Sitting at the President's right is Edwin M. Stanton, Secretary of War; standing back of him is Salmon P. Chase, Secretary of the Treasury. Seated before the table on which is placed the Emancipation Proclamation, is William H. Seward, Secretary of State, and opposite him is Gideon Wells, Secretary of the Navy. Standing back of them are (left) Caleb B. Smith, Secretary of the Interior, and Montgomery Blair, Postmaster General. Seated at extreme right is Edward Bates, United States Attorney General. The final Proclamation was issued by the President, and became effective on January 1, 1863. The act was justified as a "necessary war measure" and declared freedom of the slaves in all the states in arms against the Federal Government. Actual liberation came only by the conquest of the South by Union arms. *National Park Service.*

and brave officers and men who fought these successful battles."

Lincoln then retired and the cheering crowd, following the band, went to the residence of the Secretary of the Treasury, Salmon P. Chase. Although he assured those who greeted him that the President's act would find favor with the American people, riots in Washington indicated that many did not agree with him.

A desperate fight between white and Negro teamsters was an example of these flare-ups.

The Teamsters' Duel, sketched by Alfred R. Waud. *Library of Congress.*

Manager Lincoln. *Library of Congress.*

MANAGER LINCOLN. "Ladies and Gentlemen, I regret to say that the Tragedy, entitled *The Army of the Potomac*, has been withdrawn on account of Quarrels among the leading Performers, and I have substituted three new and striking Farces or Burlesques, one, en-titled *The Repulse at Vicksburg*, by the well-known, popular favorite, E. M. STANTON, ESQ., and the others, *The Loss of the Harriet Lane* and *The Exploits of the Alabama*—a very sweet thing in Farces, I assure you—by the Veteran Composer, GIDEON WELLES."
(*Unbounded Applause by the* COPPERHEADS.)

The Negroes were attacked by the whites with sticks, stones and knives, and driven out of their quarters. Some of the Negroes attempted to maintain their ground and one of them struck a white man with a pick, severely cut-ting his head. The whites, however, pressed the Negroes closely and, not satisfied with driving off most of them, pounced on those who had not retreated and beat them se-verely. An hour later they met again. The white teamsters, catching one of the Negroes, knocked him down, kicked him, and cut him so deeply across the abdomen that his entrails protruded. Police stayed clear of the fight and let each group take care of its own dispute. Though no one knew what had caused the trouble, and some feared that it was the be-ginning of a war to exterminate the Negroes, the general contention was that the white teamsters had been drinking too much whis-key and made the attack out of pure devilment. Similar incidents occurred when soldiers shot into another group of Negroes, wounding several of them. A New York regiment seemed to be particularly "down on the everlasting nigger" and not a colored man or woman was allowed to cross their path without being attacked.

Early in November, colored people in the District who were waiting for removal to Chiriqui in Panama sent a delegation to the White House. Congress had appropriated funds to send a colony of freed Negroes there to mine coal for the navy, and the first one hundred families to be ready were to make the trip. The delegation had a letter to the President saying that many of them had sold their furniture and given up their homes to go, but delay in their departure had reduced their scanty funds, and now that five times the original number were prepared to go, and newspapers had reported no one would be sent, they were uncertain about what was to

be done with them. They were told the President could not see them at the moment, but was anxious as ever for their departure, and had placed the matter in the hands of Senator Pomeroy, the agent of emigration. The plan was never put into effect.

Again the tax payers unloaded their grievances in the newspapers.

That Union troops in and near the city were there for its defense did not deter the population from complaining of their activities. Walks were filled with soldiers on parole or absent without leave. There was always the clank of sabers, the measured beat of marching men, and the shrill command of officers, to disturb them. Although they declared that at night, except for "rustic lanterns," the streets were in almost total darkness, and that many houses concealed spies waiting to dodge back across the river to Virginia before daylight, they protested the number of wayfarers being halted and questioned.

There was always the clank of sabers, the measured beat of marching men and the shrill command of officers to disturb Washington residents. *Library of Congress.*

Mud and dust still irritated them. One wrote: "What most is needed to contribute to the comfort and pleasure of citizens and strangers? The removal of mud and dust! This nuisance is the curse of Washington. It is as annoying as the flies of Egypt. It penetrates everywhere. It fills our carriages; it enters our houses; it spoils our clothes; it blinds our eyes; it injures our lungs; it frets our temper; it drives away strangers, in fine, it is the great plague of our lives. . . .

"That the plan of our city is a most unfortunate one I think every resident will be ready to admit and deeply regret. The streets are almost universally too wide, affording unnecessary space for the accumulation of dust, but when we add to these our immense avenues, from one hundred and sixty to two hundred feet wide—a great Sahara of dirt—the blunder of the plan is seen to be prodigious. If the space thus worse than wasted had been laid out in numerous small squares, which could be planted with trees and kept in grass, it would have been a great improvement. Let our City Council, then, awake to their duty in this respect. Let arrangements be promptly made to pave at least the more dense portions of our city. If the streets north of Pa. Av., from the Capitol to the War Department, and as far north on M street, were paved it would embrace those portions most traveled, and would do very well for a beginning. (Signed) A Tax-payer for Thirty Years."

Efforts to remedy "the great Sahara of dirt," which continued to irritate the taxpayers, brought temporary fame to citizens at various times. "Pennsylvania Avenue To Be Cleaned By Wholesale," announced one newspaper. "A machine for this purpose invented by our fellowtownsman, Mr. James P. Ellicot, was exhibited in front of the Patriotic Bank on Seventh street yesterday afternoon, in the presence of the Water Commissioners. It consists of a double perforated pipe, surmounted with a cap, and laid the entire length of the street, and in the center of the same, connected to the water mains by suitable regulators, so that any desirable amount of water can be thrown upon the street to either wash or irrigate it at pleasure. Much admiration was expressed with its performance, and the

Water Commissioners seemed satisfied of its effectiveness for general use." What became of it was a local mystery.

Meanwhile, the Emancipation Commission of the District was completing its labors in appraising the value of slaves, taking testimony as to the title and loyalty of the claimants, and compiling a final report. Claims had been presented by some 1,000 individuals in the District for 3,128 slaves, but 111 of the slaves were rejected because of disloyalty and other legal disqualifications, leaving the remainder to be paid for under the act. The Commission also granted free papers to approximately 100 slaves whose owners were disloyal or refused to present their claims.

The first case of a white man being arrested on the oath of a Negro was reported in December. The Negro, J. Short, had applied to a Justice for a warrant (which he got) against James Phumphrey whom he charged with assault and battery. Witnesses said the act was committed at Phumphrey's livery stable when the complainant neglected to perform certain work and Phumphrey asked why he had not done it. The reply he gave brought his employer's stick down on his head. The case was ruled for trial before another Justice who, not having received or seen the statute which legalized the oath of a Negro, made inquiry and was informed that Section 5 of the Supplementary Emancipation Act, approved by Congress, July 12, 1862, read: "And be it enacted that in all judicial proceedings in the District of Columbia there shall be no exclusion of any witness on account of color."

Speculations as to what the Negro would do with his birth of freedom revived a story told of Wendell Phillips, the distinguished abolitionist. While at a Southern hotel, he had his breakfast served in his room by a slave. Phillips took advantage of the opportunity to inform the Negro, in a very pathetic manner, that he was a man and a brother —and more than that—an abolitionist. The Negro, however, seemed more anxious about the breakfast than he was about their relations or the conditions of his soul. Finally, in despair, Phillips ordered him to go away, saying

A Negro jubilee, or "shout," celebrated their emancipation. *Library of Congress.*

that he couldn't bear to be waited upon by a slave. "Excuse me, Massa," said the Negro, "must stay here 'cause I'm responsible for the silverware."

There was excitement and angry debate at this time over General McClellan—his "faults" as Chief of the Union forces, and what Lincoln *should do* about relieving him of his command. A local humorist noting the arguments for and against such a change, and certain generals who might displace McClellan, explained that some thought the change should have taken place long ago so the war might be finished within the present century. Others thought the war would be finished with a vengeance now, *à la* Pope, and suggested that the people of Washington petition the President not to send McClellan too far away. In case of a Bull Run No. 3, it would be convenient to have him within call to

defend the city again. There were those who thought that Burnside had caution as well as energy and that the army would be safe in his hands while others declared that Burnside was not in the new program; Hooker was the "coming man." One who had known Hooker admitted he was a brave officer, an admirable Division Commander, but vain as a peacock —in fact, he was General Pope over again in the habit of self-laudation, and unprofessional depreciation of his superiors. Another offered to bet that with Hooker in command the Confederate army would be in Washington within a month. There were also those who believed that the President was justified in insisting on a variation upon the McClellan "strategy." They were like a traveler who, dissatisfied with the drink placed upon his dining table, shouted, "Landlord, if this is tea, bring me coffee, and if it is coffee, bring me tea, but a

111

change I will have!" And so the controversies ran on at different places of public resort, in some cases reaching a point of heat that threatened personal collisions.

In early November, General Ambrose E. Burnside superseded McClellan and the prevailing conclusion was that Lincoln, having always been a friend of McClellan, had displaced him only because a change was urgent. Of McClellan's failure to pursue the enemy when he had him on the run, Lincoln said, "He's got the slows." McClellan had let the probable capture of General Robert E. Lee and thousands of Confederate soldiers slip out of his hands at Antietam.

Now it was Burnside who was taking punishment. On December 13, a dispatch from Fredericksburg, Virginia, told of a great battle which had begun there at sunrise that morning and had closed at a quarter past six that evening. "It was desperately fought on the left. We were met by an overwhelming force, but could not be turned back." The old story, said those who knew the meaning of a wink and "To march or retreat or whatever else you choose to call it." Before Burnside could get his men across the Rappahannock River, 12,000 of them had been killed or wounded, and the clamor for his removal had begun. One month later he resigned and Hooker was given command of the Army of the Potomac.

During the holidays, the President and Mrs. Lincoln viewed the Christmas tree and decorations at the recently built Judiciary Square Hospital (which replaced the burned E Street Infirmary) for sick and wounded soldiers. As Lincoln was leaving, an elderly man remarked that, notwithstanding his extensive public duties, he "managed to hold his own." With a weary smile, Lincoln replied, "Yes, but I have not got much to hold."

The burning of Ford's Atheneum, the elegant new theatre he had recently opened, climaxed other events at this time. Within a few minutes after the alarm was given the "entire building was in flames, and presented a magnificent spectacle," read one description. "The pall of a black, stormy sky threw back the light upon the city with singular effect, and so widely illuminated the District for

miles around that people residing at the greatest distances had the impression that the fire was in their immediate neighborhood. It was not difficult to read print in the open air at almost any point within the city limits. The roof was of shingle, and the flames therefore had rapid egress, and as they shot up presented a terribly beautiful sight."

It was first supposed that the fire originated from a stove in a corner back of the stage and close to the scenery, but later it was believed that gas, escaping from a defective meter underneath the stage, had ignited. An immense crowd gathered in the vicinity of the fire, and doorsteps, tops of adjoining houses, and branches of trees were filled with people endeavoring to obtain a better view of it. But some of the curious, by meddling and getting in the way, were no help to the firemen. Neither was the steam fire-engine "Hibernia" which got stuck in the mud and was delayed in arriving. Within three quarters of an hour nothing was left of the theatre but its blackened walls. Several small frame dwellings nearby were burned to the ground and many articles were stolen by those pretending to save them. The light-fingered gentry were busy too, and not a few pockets were picked. One spectator at least did not remain until the fire was extinguished. While it was raging he remarked that the fire was a judgment from heaven for converting a church into a theatre. The answers he got from bystanders made it wise for him to leave the locality. Other than John Ford, then in Baltimore, the heaviest losers were the Richings, whose entire theatrical wardrobe was destroyed, and the Ronzani Ballet Troup who lost all its possessions. But a greater tragedy awaited Ford in the theatre he was to rebuild on the smoldering ruins of that December evening holocaust.

The President's New Year's reception at noon swarmed with civilians, the military, and the police—the latter there to take care of the light-fingered gentry sauntering among the crowd. The scramble for hats and coats left many visitors with strange attire, and some took away torn clothing on their own bruised bodies when they left. The gayety of the New Year celebrations, however, was not enhanced by the early news from Murfreesborough, Tennessee. "GREATEST CARNAGE OF THE WAR," it read, "Our Entire Army Suffered Terribly. Four Regiments Of Regulars Lost Half Of Their Men And All Their Commanding Officers." Two days later a dispatch from Grant to the War Department brought out better headlines: "GLORIOUS NEWS FROM TENNESSEE. SPLENDID UNION VICTORY. Rebels Whipped Completely. Driven From Murfreesborough In Full Retreat. Our Forces Pursuing." But the victory, with its countless casualties, failed to lift Washington out of the doldrums.

The Emancipation Proclamation (for the abolition of slavery in subjected states), issued on the first day of the New Year (1863), renewed the controversy about Negroes in the District. Disputes continued to arise among Washington residents as to what should be done to make them aware of their new responsibilities so they could become self-supporting and not a burden to the community. One endeavored to explain why the Negroes "not long in our midst" astonished the white people by their unreasonable demands. He had asked a former slave how the colored people in the District would provide for themselves, and the old Negro had replied, "Master gave all his people food, without having anything to pay for it. Our bacon and meal was always here; about this we had no care. Now we certainly expect the Union people to do as well by us as our masters did in Dixie. Once a year our masters gave out clothing among the people, and it was free—we had nothing to pay for it. We expect the Union people to do more for us than our southern masters. Besides, the slave had his rights. He was permitted to have his own poultry yard and truck patch, and by most masters he was allowed to keep a pig, and could do over-work for his own pay when his master's work was done."

Negro celebrations of their emancipation soon became a Washington problem. Being free to go their own way, they began by fighting among themselves. A large ballroom near the Capitol was the arena for some of these battles-royal. Frequently the riots ended in bloodshed. According to one report: "The ballroom was densely packed with ebonyites —so much so that all dancing was prevented— who amused themselves in pummeling each others' heads until the arrival of the police, when the riot was suppressed. After a short breathing spell, however, the darkies went at it again, and upon the police rushing into the room they extinguished the lights and rushed upon Sergeant Milstead and Patrolman Simonds. One of them attempted to stab Patrolman Simonds. Fortunately the blow fell short of its mark, and he escaped with no further injury than the cutting of his uniform. Citizens being called to the assistance of the police, the ballroom was quickly cleared of the belligerents and order was restored. Balls are frequently held in this house by the colored people, and the disorder has been carried to an extent which has elicited general complaint from the residents of the neighborhood. It has become a den for riot and rowdyism, and we hope hereafter the police will refuse permits for these entertainments."

The police also conducted another Washington "house cleaning" about this time. "GRAND EXODUS OF FEMALES RICHMOND-WARD," reported the press. "Among Cyprians thus 'swarming off' from the hives here are delegations from various noted establishments about town: Sal Austin's No. 10 Marble Alley, The Iron-Clad Battery, Fort Sumter, The Monitor, Headquarters U.S.A., Gentle Annie Lyles, and The Cottage By The Sea."

The arrival of "General" Tom Thumb (Charles E. Stratton) and his bride (Lavinia Warren) in February drew the attention of the public. He was twenty-four years old, thirty-two inches high, and weighed twenty-one pounds. She was four years younger, of the same height, and eight pounds heavier. Only a few weeks before, the "distinguished Lilliputians" had been married in New York City, and P. T. Barnum, super-showman of the day who had the "General" under contract, had lost no time in publicizing the event and arranging to have the couple presented to chiefs of republics and royal sovereigns.

At the White House, they met the President

Tom Thumb and his wife (Mr. and Mrs. Charles E. Stratton). *N.Y. Public Library.*

and Mrs. Lincoln whose other guests included the Cabinet and many government officials, nearly all of whom brought their families with them. The "General" wore a "full suit of black, patent-leather boots, a faultless necktie, a large breast pin of brilliants, a gold watch with an elaborate chain, and a pair of snow-white kid gloves." His diminutive wife was gowned in rich, white satin, sprinkled with green leaves and looped with carnation buds, with a necklace, cluster pin, and bracelets of sparkling diamonds unmatched by any woman attending the affair.

Lincoln remarked to the "General" that he had put the President of the United States "completely in the shade" for since his arrival in the capital he had been "the greater center of attraction." Mrs. Tom Thumb said that she was devoted to the Union cause and was willing for the "General" to volunteer if necessary. Refreshments were served which "the little folks appeared to relish as much as any one present." They returned to the Willard Hotel where they promenaded through the hall to the ballroom and, with other members of their suite, danced a quadrille to the music of Goodall's Capital Band before retiring to their apartment. The following morning they left for Philadelphia.

114

Washington was now hearing of another "General" who had been given the name of "Mud." Returning soldiers spoke of the attempt to inaugurate a genuine winter campaign as a disastrous failure. Union forces, they said, had been defeated by "General Mud" before a gun was fired. "It was terrible," one soldier said, "mud up to our horses' bellies and up to our guns' axletrees." Troops, soaked through with rain, stood shivering in the cold for hours, or floundered through the mud, often knee deep. Men had the seeds of disease implanted in them and horses had to be shot. Another soldier told of Hooker's army having retreated, after heavy casualties, and returned to its former camp on the northern bank of the Rappahannock River. The army was safe, but with ten thousand fewer men in its ranks, and a much larger number unfit for duty. The heavy rain and the chilling atmosphere had severely impaired the health of the troops who were wholly without means of shelter. The tents were left behind, and many lost their knapsacks and other possessions in battle.

One day's arrival of wounded in Washington numbered almost eight hundred of Hooker's men. Some were brought in by boat and the Seventh Street cars, which ran to the river, were requisitioned to assist the ambulances in removing them. War records showed that absentees and deserters of the Union army were upward of 125,000 men. In April it was announced that the date fixed by the proclamation of the President for their voluntary return, without punishment, had expired and they were to be classed and punished as deserters.

Lincoln's request that the last day of the month be set apart as a "National Fast Day" was "more generally observed than any previous occasion of the kind ever known here," reported the press. All shops were closed and residents were asked to gather at places of worship to pray for "the restoration of our now divided and suffering country to its former happy condition of unity and peace."

During the first week of May, the Washington *Star* seemed reluctant to comment freely on the activity of General Hooker in his attempt to storm Richmond and Chancellorsville. "We have scrupulously refrained from giving publicity to any of the late movements of General Hooker, and in accordance with what was understood to be the wishes of the Government, did not reproduce what had appeared in the Northern newspapers. As the *Chronicle* and *Intelligencer* (other Washington newspapers) have now given their full ventilation, nothing can be gained by withholding the same information from our readers. While giving these details of what has already transpired, we shall carefully avoid furnishing anything of what is occurring in the present or likely to in the future, calculated to afford any possible information to the enemy, and trust that our contemporaries will be guided by the same sense of duty. In the present encouraging position of affairs we can well afford to wait a short season for the full development of the plans of General Hooker, which have thus far been carried out with such brilliant success." Soon the press was again trying to explain "the causes of retreat."

The *Star's* concern was of little value to the owner and editor, W. D. Wallach, a month later when he was indicted and charged "with treason in the publication of news alleged to be contraband," and a warrant was issued for his arrest. He had published a letter giving the particulars of Hooker's recent movement and position which also had appeared in the newspapers of Northern cities. Although it was contended that the news was "as common as goose pasture," all the papers which had published the letter were threatened with prosecution. The Government was beginning to crack down on the release of war information.

Then came John Wilkes Booth for his first stage appearance in Washington. Although Mrs. Lincoln was seeking the advice of well-known spiritualists in the city, none warned her of this thespian, particularly adept with a pistol. Announced as the pride of the American people and youngest tragedian in the world, the dapper actor opened his engagement at Grover's Theatre in *Richard III*. Reviews were flattering and the younger brother of the famous Edwin Booth played to well-filled houses. Men and women boasted of his

friendship and liked to be seen in public places with him. His dark eyes and curly black hair, enhanced by a pale skin, a handsome figure and immaculate dress, made him one of the outstanding personalities strutting the streets of Washington. His sympathies, however, were with the Confederacy and he did not hesitate to speak in its behalf at every opportunity. Had he not had so many qualities in his favor—a name already famous, social support and popularity in general—he might have been hustled off to the Old Capitol Prison in due payment for his vitriolic tirades against Lincoln and the Federal Government.

During this engagement Wilkes gave some of his best performances. Any misfortune attending the Union forces seemed to have a good effect upon him. "Although constantly interfered with by the same causes which have troubled the army of the Potomac, bad weather and rain," one review said, "yet the young tragedian has played with all his accustomed fire; and his audiences have been always appreciative, and generally large." A fair share of good notices and box office returns encouraged Wilkes to take over the Washington Theatre as lessee, manager, and star, but news of Union defeats lessened

A portrait of John Wilkes Booth from a painting in the possession of the author.

Photograph of Lincoln taken at about this time by Alexander Gardner, formerly employed by Mathew Brady.

patronage at public places, and his venture was not successful.

On the heels of Wilkes' engagement, policeman John F. Parker got into the news. On this occasion Parker was guilty of less than failing to guard Lincoln at Ford's Theatre on the night of the assassination. Parker's case had to do with beating a Negro corporal and tearing off his chevrons. After arresting the Negro for disturbing the peace, the Negro had called him a "white sonofabitch" and Parker had taken the matter into his own hands. Parker was brought before a captain of the Military Governor's staff who curtly told him that "whatever might be the private opinion of anyone, the Government having authorized the raising of colored soldiers, they should be treated as soldiers."

Two obscure men in Washington at this time were marked for fame later in life. They lived and worked, as thousands of others did, on small pay and hopes of better government jobs. One was six feet tall, rather robust, but having a soft white skin, ruddy complexion, slightly gray hair and a full beard. He survived from day to day in an unkempt room where he scribbled articles and poems, wrote letters for soldiers, cared for their needs as best he could, and roamed the streets absorbing its people, sights, pulsations, and all else the city offered. His name was Walt Whitman. His companion on many of these jaunts, and on quiet evenings and Sunday breakfasts, was a less conspicuous man with dark hair, thin beard and mustache, and a boyish face, who was interested in bird life and nature in fields, parks, woods, and other nearby places where the army was not holding forth. His name was John Burroughs, a Treasury Department clerk. Some of the events which they witnessed during war years of that period were recorded in their writings. One by Whitman described Lincoln as he saw him in the summer of 1863:

"I see the President almost every day, as I happen to live where he passes to or from his lodgings out of town. He never sleeps at the White House during the summer season, but has quarters at a healthy location some three miles north of the city, the Soldiers'

Walt Whitman. *National Archives.*

John Burroughs. *Courtesy of the Burroughs family.*

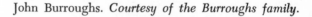

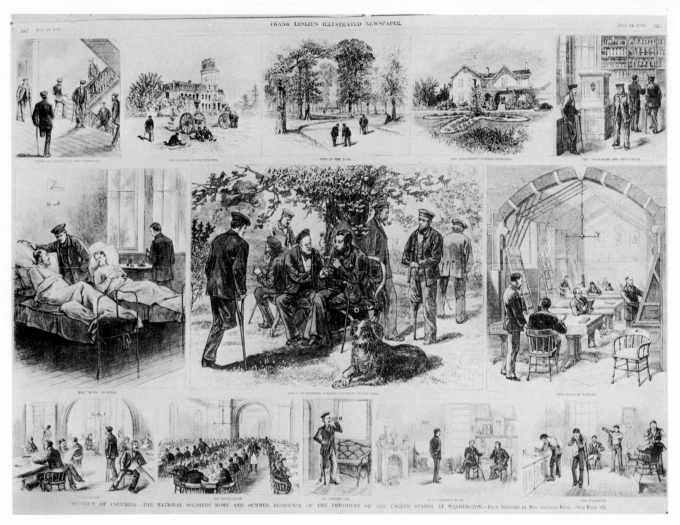

DISTRICT OF COLUMBIA—THE NATIONAL SOLDIERS HOME AND SUMMER RESIDENCE OF THE PRESIDENT OF THE UNITED STATES, AT WASHINGTON.—From Sketches by Miss Georgie Davis.—See Page 351.

Views of the Soldiers' Home showing the cottage occupied by the President during the summer months. *Library of Congress.*

Home, a United States military establishment. . . . He always has a company of twenty-five or thirty cavalry, with sabres drawn and held upright over their shoulders. They say this guard was against his personal wish, but he let his counselors have their way. The party makes no great show in uniform or horses. Mr. Lincoln on the saddle generally rides a good-sized, easy-going gray horse, is dress'd in plain black, somewhat rusty and dusty, wears a black stiff hat, and looks about as ordinary in attire, etc., as the commonest man. A lieutenant, with yellow straps, rides at his

left, and following behind, two by two, come the cavalry men, in their yellow-striped jackets. They are generally going at a slow trot, as that is the pace set them by the one they wait upon. The sabres and accoutrements clank, and the entirely unornamental *cortège* as it trots toward Lafayette Square arouses no sensation, only some curious stranger stops and gazes. I see very plainly Abraham Lincoln's dark brown face, with the deep-cut lines, the eyes, always to me with a deep latent sadness in the expression. We have got so that we exchange bows, and very cordial ones. Sometimes the President goes and comes in an open barouche. The cavalry always accompany him, with drawn sabres. Often I notice as he goes out evenings—and sometimes in the morning, when he comes early—he turns off and halts at the large and handsome residence of the Secretary of War, on K street, and holds conference there. If in his barouche, I can see from my window he does not alight, but sits in his vehicle, and Mr. Stanton comes out to attend him. Sometimes one of his sons, a boy of ten or twelve, accompanies him, riding at his right on a pony. Earlier in the summer I occasionally saw the President and his wife, toward the latter part of the afternoon, out in a barouche, on a pleasure ride through the city. Mrs. Lincoln was dress'd in complete black, with a long crêpe veil. The equipage is of the plainest kind, only two horses, and they nothing extra. They pass'd me once very close, and I saw the President in the face fully, as they were moving slowly, and his look, though abstracted, happen'd to be directed steadily in my eye. He bow'd and smiled, but far beneath his smile I noticed well the expression I have alluded to. None of the artists or pictures has caught the deep, though subtle and indirect expression of this man's face. There is something else there. One of the great portrait painters of two or more centuries ago is needed." Occasionally Lincoln

Tad Lincoln on the pony he rode when he accompanied his father to and from the Soldiers' Home. *Library of Congress.*

The open barouche used by Lincoln in Washington. *National Park Service.*

119

Stuntz's Fancy Store, 1207 New York Avenue, Northwest, where Lincoln took his son Tad to buy toys. *Columbia Historical Society.*

The New York Avenue Presbyterian Church, often attended by the President and his family. *Washington Public Library.*

stopped at Stuntz's Toy Shop to make purchases for Tad who was fond of tin and wooden soldiers in bright colors, and other miniature-war playthings.

Noah Brooks, newsman and friend of "the rising prairie lawyer" in Illinois, came to Washington in 1862 and often attended the New York Avenue Presbyterian Church, a favorite place of worship for the President. There Brooks "took a long look" at him and described the change in his personal appearance as "marked and sorrowful. His eyes were almost deathly in their gloomy depths, and on his visage was an air of profound sadness. His face was colorless and drawn, and newly grown whiskers added to the agedness of his appearance. When I had seen him last in Illinois, his face, although always sallow, wore a tinge of rosiness in the cheeks, but now it was pale and lifeless."

Late in June, with Grant's attempt to seize Vicksburg, came the startling news of Lee's invasion of Pennsylvania, and that his army, "100,000 strong," was crossing the Potomac. Reports on the following day told of hundreds of horses being driven over the bridges of the Susquehanna River, followed by fleeing men, women, and children, as the rebels moved toward Gettysburg. Alarm spread over the capital; its defense was discussed everywhere. Said the press: "As it may be possible that the movements of the rebels North may require more troops at this point sooner or later, it seems to us that it would be well for the Government to call out the District Militia for as long as may be necessary to complete their organization thoroughly, and at the same time familiarize them with the duty of such service as may eventually be required of them in rifle-pits and elsewhere in and around the fortifications surrounding Washington." It also suggested that by proclaiming martial law throughout the District, and conscripting all strangers who were within the ages required for bearing arms, some 20,000 men might be added to the service.

As the rebel invasion continued to march into Pennsylvania, Lincoln relieved Hooker and put General George G. Meade in command of the Army of the Potomac. Newspapers, in an effort to keep up with events, gave staccato reports of the armies lining up for battle. "EXTRA! Lee Concentrating His Army In The Valley Between Shippensburg And Chambersburg, Evidently Anticipating An Attack From The Army Of The Potomac. General Meade Cuts The Rebel Lines In Two. A Great Battle Imminent." On the following day a report from Harrisburg told of very rapid and heavy firing heard there in the direction of Carlisle some distance away: "The river banks are lined with persons listening and discussing the possible results."

Again news poured from the press. Editions were grabbed by anxious residents as soon as they reached the streets. "EXTRA! EXTRA! Stirring News From Pennsylvania! A Terrible Battle! Our Forces Successfully Resisting! Rebel Corps Of Longstreet And Hill Attacked Our 1st And 11th Army Corps Under Generals Reynolds And Meade On Road Between Gettysburg And Chambersburg. Battle Very Severe. Our Losses Heavy, Including General Reynolds Killed." For the first time during the war, a battle was taking place upon the soil of a free state—at Gettysburg.

Next day came the news that Major John S. Mosby's rebel guerrillas (engaged in irregular warfare) were on the rampage in the vicinity of Washington. They were looting houses, had captured Union General E. H. Stoughton and some prisoners from the very midst of the army, had stolen a Negro family, and taken over the Fairfax Courthouse as headquarters. Once more the rebels were too close for comfort, and the President ordered Major Gen-

Major John S. Mosby (center, wearing feather in hat) and his "Guerrillas" were known as a hard-riding band of looters whose exploits often terrorized Washington and nearby communities. *National Archives.*

July 6, 1863, *Star*.

122

eral George C. Thomas to immediately muster into service eight regiments of the District Militia for sixty days "unless exigencies sooner pass away."

To assure anyone doubting what was in store for the guerrillas when caught, the press commented: "The general orders respecting guerrillas are very pointed. We quote some of them: Secretary Stanton says: 'Let them swing.' Gen. Dix advises to 'shoot them on the spot.' Gen. Schofield says, 'Execute them immediately.' Gen. Blunt says, 'Give them no quarter.' Gen. Logan says, 'Shoot them when found.' Gen. Halleck's orders are, 'Let them be tried immediately by a drumhead court, and punished with death.'"

Fears were calmed by news from Pennsylvania which indicated that Meade was succeeding and, according to the press, "bids fair to use up Lee's army before our patriotic citizens, upon whom the call was made [for service in the militia] will be able to get a glimpse of a rebel in arms." The prediction was correct. Two days later headlines read: "EXTRA! EXTRA! Great And Glorious News! Union Arms Victorious In The Greatest Battle Of The Century! Lee's Retreat Certain Unless Willing To Risk Annihilation Of His Army! EXTRA! EXTRA! Lee's Army Retreating Toward Potomac! Many Captured In Famished Condition! EXTRA! EXTRA! Army Of The Potomac Advanced And Occupied Gettysburg Without Opposition!"

Excitement over Lee's defeat at Gettysburg during the three days' battle, Meade's capture of thousands of Confederate soldiers and routing the rebel forces, grew as Grant's prediction that he would eat his Fourth of July dinner in Vicksburg proved to be true. Hopes were renewed that the war was near an end, and the city celebrated with parades, bands, and a serenade to Lincoln. Everywhere there was wild rejoicing.

Later reports of Lee stated that his retreat had been checked by the rise of the Potomac, but a small portion of his transportation had crossed on rafts at Williamsport and Shoppardstown, and that his stock had been able to swim over. "His ambulance trains with wounded have also crossed," it continued, "but his supply trains, artillery, infantry and cavalry are reported to be all on this side. His first line of battle has been formed on the Antietam fields. Should this prove true, and it is certain that he cannot receive reinforcements, he will be compelled to trust the fate of his army to arbitrament of a bloody field. Our forces are gradually penetrating in the direction, and the next few hours are pregnant with the fate of thousands and the welfare of our country. Hopes of annihilating the entire rebel army of Virginia are bright." But the deal did not come off and residents continued to read newspaper accounts of other battles, movement of troops, invasions, and—General Lee.

As the President awaited news from Gettysburg, Mrs. Lincoln was brought back to the White House, bruised and suffering a head injury when she jumped from her carriage during a runaway. As the carriage passed an open lot near the Mount Pleasant Hospital, the coachman's seat suddenly became detached and fell to the ground taking the driver with it. Immediately the horses dashed off with Mrs. Lincoln alone in the carriage, "but seeing the imminent danger she was in, with courage and presence of mind remarkable at so critical a moment, [she] sprang quickly from the carriage while the horses were running at full speed." Though stunned for a moment, the most serious injury from the fall,

Mount Pleasant Hospital at Fourteenth Street Northwest above Boundary (Florida Avenue) showing flag marked "H", the large number of tents for "overflow" sick and wounded, and an army wagon used for carrying medical supplies. *National Archives.*

Soldiers' rest and train leaving the nearby railroad station where pickpockets were hustled out of Washington. *National Archives.*

other than the bruises, was a gash on the back of her head from which the blood flowed freely. Several surgeons, called from the hospital, arrived instantly and took care of her. When it was found that no bones had been broken, she was taken back to the White House.

Inundations on the Washington-New York railroad delayed passengers, mails, and out-of-town newspapers, and the situation in which the city again found itself brought letters to local editors in answer to certain accusations made by them. B. B. French,

Commissioner of Public Buildings, wrote in part: "Some of the city papers have recently chosen to call to account 'the public authorities having charge of the streets'—meaning, I suppose, the Mayor and myself—for suffering the overflow of the streets, the wooden crossings to be washed away and the mud to accumulate, etc. I wonder they do not call to account the powers far above either the Mayor or the Commissioner for opening the windows of heaven and pouring down the uncommon floods of rain that have recently not only inundated our streets here, but

washed away the permanent and substantial stone bridges of the Baltimore and Ohio Railroad Company, and interrupted the travel between here and Baltimore for days. . . ."

Travel was not delayed for pickpockets and thieves who were given a parade before their departure. Said the press: "Another cleaning out of disreputable characters took place today, by the drumming through and out of the city thirteen pickpockets, thieves and vagrants generally, who had been in confinement in the Central Guardhouse." They had been lined up under a guard and marched to the corner of Pennsylvania Avenue and Tenth Street, "where a halt was made, and the large crowd who had been attracted by the curious sight, availed themselves of the opportunity to take a good look at the 'mugs' of the gang. The drum and fife then struck up the 'Rogue's March' and the party, followed by a curious crowd of men and boys, were marched along Pennsylvania Avenue to Seventeenth Street, down the latter street past the War Department, and then back again to the Avenue, and thence to the depot, where they are to be placed on the cars, and given a free ride North—we hope never to return. The crowd is about as hard looking an one as has yet been drummed out. They stared about them with brazen boldness, and there was not one who seemed pained at being compelled to wear a red badge labeled 'pickpocket and thief.' Among this party are George D. Cassidy and Robert Jarvis, the ringleaders in the late attempt to escape from the guardhouse."

At the depot "they were paraded alongside of the train, and as soon as the large number of soldiers who were nearby at the Soldiers' Rest caught a glimpse of them, they were groaned and hooted at vociferously. One of the soldiers recognized among them one who had once rolled him, and just as the train moved off he thrust his fist in the window and gave Mr. Pick a powerful blow as a slight testament of his regard. Some of the soldiers were very indignant against them, and one officer in particular cursed them in good style, when one of the rogues sang out, 'Never mind, you sonofabitch, many a pocket you've helped

to pick with me.' As soon as the train moved off, the soldiers mockingly cheered them, and several of the rogues in a very dignified manner bowed their acknowledgments to the supposed compliment."

Reports under Local News told of other police activities. "The Bake Oven Burnt Out" described how police officers of the Tenth Precinct had descended upon "the house known as Madam Russell's Bake Oven, on D Street south, near Seventh street, and captured Mary Hartman, alias Madam Russell, the reputed keeper of the house, and the girls living there. All were taken before a Justice Ferguson, but since it could not be proved who kept the house, they were all dismissed on condition that they vacate the premises."

The police were also having trouble near the Ambulance Park with a young woman, Anna Lang, who was putting on "an uncommon exhibition. She was very drunk and quite without clothing (except shoes and stockings), and minus even that fine robe of chastity which art critics tell us suffices to drape such nude figures as 'The Greek Slave.' The officers found a crowd of men and boys admiring her figure, which was quite neat, except that it approached the Humphrey Marshall style. The boys were at once driven off and the officers arrested her, but she proved to be a regular termagent, and the police found it as difficult to keep a blanket over her as to ward off the admiring gaze of the bystanders, and sent for an ambulance and she was taken to the stationhouse, where it took six men to carry her in and lock her up, she tearing the clothes off some of them, who had to carry her by the arms, legs and head. Justice Drury fined her $2, and ordered her to be locked up, but some of her friends subsequently brought her clothes and paid her fine, and she started immediately for the camps. It was stated that her clothes having become dirty, she took them off and gave them to a teamster to have them washed, and tried to hide meanwhile in the bushes, but she became too noisy to be kept in one place. She has been before the police heretofore, and also has served eighteen months as a soldier."

Late July found Washington still struggling

LADY CLERKS LEAVING THE TREASURY DEPARTMENT AT WASHINGTON.—[SKETCHED BY A. R. WAUD.]

PENNSYLVANIA AVENUE TO BE
CLEANED. The unsightly and disagreeable filthy masses of mud now to be seen along Pennsylvania Avenue, are to be removed. The citizens along that thoroughfare have taken the matter in hand, and having obtained a detail of laborers from the contraband camp, the work of scraping up the mud preparatory to being carted off, was vigorously commenced yesterday. After the scrapings are hauled off, Mr. Critcherson's sweeping machine will be employed to keep the avenue clean."

At this time citizens also complained of "The Prevailing Sickness" and the press, under that caption, published a letter from one who noted that "Dr. Stone and other distinguished physicians are unanimous in their opinion that the burning of so many bodies of animals during the night is the cause of a vast amount of sickness, partly owing to the fact that some of these bodies are putrid, and all of them ing the affluvia is carried along with the smoke, and, settling over the city, the murky poison rushes through every open window, and makes the unwary sleepers victims to its baneful influence. The prospect is that if this disease-making process is continued a few nights more, there will be a far greater number of names enrolled on the sick list than for the conscript service."

August brought the opening of Ford's New Theatre with the romantic spectacle of *The Naiad Queen*. The interior was spacious and elegantly furnished and its exterior compared favorably with other public buildings. Being a square from the Avenue, and on higher ground, it had the advantage of light, air, and drainage. John Ford was again on his way to fame and fortune in the theatrical world, but it was only a matter of time until more calamity would be brought upon him by John Wilkes Booth in that very theatre.

It was at Wilkes' first engagement there in

Opposite above:
Employees leaving the Treasury Department Building in the rain. Note the wide wooden plank used for crossing the street at extreme right. *Library of Congress.*

Left:
The Fourteenth Massachusetts Regiment marching up Pennsylvania Avenue in a storm. *Library of Congress.*

Right:
Ford's Theatre on Tenth Street between E and F Streets, Northwest, showing condition of the street and carriage-blocks used at entrances. The sign at curb advertises Kimmel's Steam House.

John Wilkes Booth, playing the leading role of Raphael Duchalet in *The Marble Heart* at Ford's new theatre on the night Lincoln attended the performance. Drawing to illustrate the author's article in the *Washington Sunday Star,* April 13, 1941.

November that Lincoln heartily applauded the young actor in *The Marble Heart*. When told of it, Wilkes remarked that he would rather have had the applause of a Negro. Also informed that the President had ex-

pressed a desire to meet him, Wilkes treated the compliment with silence. John Hay, the President's assistant private secretary, who accompanied him that evening described the play as "rather tame than otherwise." But there was reason for Lincoln's applause; the press always noted that Wilkes' performance in *The Marble Heart* was one of his best efforts. Romantic parts were more suitable for his fine physique and talent than the roles of prelates or ranting old men. What he saw in the capital, however, probably increased his hatred of the North, or amused his vanity in thinking of himself as a Beau Brummel and devotee of Southern chivalry.

The frequent appearance of paroled rebel officers, wearing their uniforms and swaggering in public places, brought verbal outbursts and threats from Union soldiers and loyal residents, and encouragement to newsboys and bootblacks who pelted such effrontry with mud and pebbles. The fear that rebel spies might be planning havoc in the city resulted in the arrest and questioning of many loyal citizens. Wilkes Booth was not among them, but Walt Whitman, going about in his open-

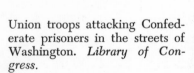

Union troops attacking Confederate prisoners in the streets of Washington. *Library of Congress.*

Lincoln with his secretaries, John George Nicolay and John Hay. *Library of Congress.*

collar shirt, lace cuffs, long gray hair and beard, and natural ruddy complexion, was picked up by a federal officer who thought he was a spy in masquerade and his face painted.

Among the local items that month one stated that "President Lincoln has not drawn his salary for the past year from the Treasury. When reminded by friends that by putting the same upon interest he would receive an income of at least twelve hundred dollars, he replied that he thought that the United States needed the use of the money quite as much as any person, and he would let it remain."

Reports of a great battle near Chickamauga, where Union lines were wavering, rebels cheering the advance of their troops, and the fighting was bloody, were followed by a call for 300,000 more volunteers. Arrests of army deserters, disorderly soldiers, rebel spies, seizures of property by the Marshal of the District under the confiscation act, riots in the various alley domains, fights between white and Negro teamsters (who were at each other's throats again), raids on gambling dens, whore houses, illegal barrooms, ferreting out counterfeiters and persons forging discharge papers and selling them to soldiers, set a lively pace in Washington that winter. The clamor for reform found the Sons of Temperance celebrating the twenty-first anniversary of the organizations in the city. When they

The last ditch at last, a cartoon in *Harper's Weekly*. *Library of Congress.*

THE LAST DITCH AT LAST.—Scene near Corinth.

marched to the White House, led by the Marine Band, the President invited them into the East Room where speakers declaimed against drunkenness in the Union forces.

Apparently Lincoln was somewhat amused by the request that he sober the Union army for he answered: "You have suggested that in an army—our army—drunkenness is a great evil, and one which, while it exists to a very great extent, we cannot expect to overcome so entirely as to leave such success in our arms as we might have without it. This undoubtedly is true, and while it is perhaps rather a bad source to derive comfort from, nevertheless, in a hard struggle, I do not know but what it is some consolation to be aware that there is some intemperance on the other side too, and that they have no right to beat us in physical combat on that ground. . . . I thank you very heartily, gentlemen, for this call, and for bringing with you these very many pretty ladies." After E. W. Dunbar had sung his opus, "We Are Coming, Father Abraham, Three Hundred Thousand More," the crowd proceeded to the Hall of the Smithsonian Institution and continued their harangue against the evils of liquor.

The opening of the new National Race Course for the fall season took on the color of a grand review with soldiers, officers, and dignitaries attending. It was located on high ground, now the site of St. Elizabeth's Hospital, which gave a fine view of the city. Purses were high and rivalry was keen on the track and in the grandstand where the betting was heavy. The great trotting race, however, had to be postponed because of a storm. Under favorable skies it was run in mile heats, best three in five, for a purse of a thousand dollars, given by the proprietor of the course. Thousands of spectators saw Butler win over Prince by half a neck in the fourth heat. Smaller tracks, such as the one near the John Peter Van Ness mansion, where the Pan-American building stands today, were also well patronized regardless of booming guns and war reports.

On August 1 the press had announced the purchase by the United States Government of the part of the Gettysburg battlefield where

Lincoln, photographed by Gardner four days before making his address at Gettysburg. Envelope containing a copy of speech to be made by Senator Edward Everett is on the table beside him. *Library of Congress.*

the desperate attack had been made upon the left center of the Union army. It was to be converted into a national cemetery. Consecration of the battlefield took Lincoln and high officials from Washington to the ceremonies in mid-November. The Honorable Edward Everett, orator for the occasion, read a long speech while the President spoke only a few words and returned to Washington. Newspapers devoted much space to Everett's oration, but history imbedded Lincoln's few words in bronze.

The same engine and coach, now the President's car, which brought Lincoln most of the way from Springfield to Washington, and on which he made the round trip for the celebration at Gettysburg, was to carry him again over the long journey back to Illinois as the nation's first martyred President. *Library of Congress.*

The dome of the Capitol awaits the arrival of the Statue of Freedom. *National Archives.*

The names of Chattanooga, Lookout Mountain, Missionary Ridge, Sherman and Grant, now ran through press reports under headings, "GREAT AND GLORIOUS NEWS. Rebels Retreating. Every Attempt Of The Enemy To Regain Possessions Gallantly Repulsed. Our Success Complete. Victory! Victory!" And once again the prediction was made that "The end is approaching, as all must now see on this eventful Thanksgiving Day." But other names were waiting for their place in history, and the citizens of Washington were yet to experience their greatest fear of invasion by the rebel army.

Interest was now centered on completion of the Capitol dome. The gigantic figure, described by the press as "The Star of Freedom," cast in bronze by Clark Mills from a model by Thomas Crawford made in Italy, had been hoisted into place and topped by a flagstaff. As one hundred guns boomed from the east side of the Capitol grounds, bands played, people shouted, and the Star Spangled Banner was raised to signify the end of the work.

Statue of Freedom. *National Park Service.*

132

Jefferson Davis, as Secretary of War in the Cabinet of Franklin Pierce, had made the final selection in its design. He had replaced the original headdress denoting Liberty with a plumed helmet surrounded by stars, and Lincoln had not changed it.

The introduction of water from the Potomac River into the city was steered by the Council into another notable event. On December 4 they assembled at the City Hall and proceeded in carriages to Great Falls, some fifteen miles distant, where they were joined by Secretary of the Interior, John Usher, and other distinguished civilians, and shown the new waterworks. After the water had been turned on, speeches were made by Mr. Usher and Mayor Wallach. An explanation of the former water supply revealed that "The aqueduct water now used in this city does not come from the Potomac, but from supplies by water courses struck along the line of the aqueduct this side of Great Falls. So this is really the celebration of the first introduction of the Potomac water into the city." The party later attended a dinner at the National Hotel at which the Mayor said: "From this day forth those who drink good liquor will have good water to go with it; and those of us who drink water only will have good water for that purpose."

This span of the aqueduct system crossing the Potomac River at Georgetown was drained during the Civil War and used as a bridge by Union troops. *Columbia Historical Society.*

Crowd at the Pennsylvania Avenue entrance to the Capitol grounds on the daily adjournment of Congress. *Library of Congress.*

Russian naval officers are guests of the United States Government in Washington. *Library of Congress.*

The opening of Congress and reception for officers of the Russian fleet visiting the city, ushered in the holidays. Upon arrival, the four Russian vessels exchanged salutes with the United States Navy Yard guns, and anchored in the river between the city and Alexandria. Baron Edward de Stoeckl, the Russian Minister, took the brilliantly decorated officers in tow and squired them to a series of gay parties, including one given by the United States Secretary of the Navy. They were received at the White House by the President and high-ranking officials, with a bevy of beautiful women to smile upon them. Newspapers reported that "everything passed off pleasantly." In return, the Russians invited United States officials to visit the fleet, and Baron de Stoeckl called upon the President to thank him for the kindness extended to his countrymen while in the capital.

Their visit was marked by another great horse stampede with three thousand animals running wildly through the streets, compelling hundreds of citizens and soldiers to scour the city in an effort to recover them. Completion of the large government stables at Giesboro Point, farther out in the District, greatly relieved the congestion and dangers caused by the frantic animals within the city. Raids on whiskey shops demanded equal fortitude and ingenuity, as well as drastic action, on the part of a patrol under orders from the Provost Marshal. They tore down a number of little shanties on New Jersey Avenue in the vicinity of the depot, declaring it was the only way to stop the sale of whiskey to soldiers since the occupants had been repeatedly fined.

The President's reception on New Year's Day brought the usual large crowd to the White House. At noon, members of the Cabinet, Judges of the Supreme Court, foreign ministers, military officers, V.I.P.s of Washington, and innumerable fluttering females, began arriving. The President wore a plain black suit and white kid gloves, while Mrs. Lincoln was elegantly gowned in satin, lace, and costly jewelry. After being presented to the President and Mrs. Lincoln, the guests passed through adjoining rooms to a large window from which a wooden platform led to the grounds. Canvas had been spread over the rich carpets to protect them from mud and dirt, for once the formalities were concluded, the gates to the grounds were thrown open, and a general rush was made by persons eager to be first in the receiving line. Heels and toes were trampled upon and considerable damage was done to hats, bonnets, and fine dresses. Even the Marine Band, as it played, was in danger of being run over. Pickpockets went to work "lifting wallets," some reported to have contained several hundred dollars.

Once more the press was warned to curb some of the war news. The Provost General of the Army of the Potomac had issued an order prohibiting newspaper correspondents with the army from publishing, or causing to be published, the names of regiments and the number of men who had enlisted or were absent on furlough. There also was an order for the enrollment of civilians with the army, some of whom had taken refuge in Union camps to avoid the draft. A hint of what was in store for Washington followed:

"Both the public and our own private advices indicate that the rebels under Gen. Early are preparing for another movement in the Shenandoah Valley. Assurances at the same time are given that ample precautions have been taken to make certain that the rebels will be able to effect nothing; but Winchester and Harper's Ferry have so often been the scene of reverses to us just after such assurances have been given, that we always feel apprehensive in relation to our military affairs there. With no immediate pressure of the enemy on us at any other point, we ought, however, at this time, to be fully prepared for any manifestation they may make in the valley." Their anxiety was well-founded: Early was planning to attack Fort Stevens, formerly Fort Massachusetts, a short distance north from Washington on the Seventh Street Road. It was now one of the city's main defenses.

To glorify their first anniversary of freedom, the Negroes held an "Emancipation Jubilee" at the Union League Hall, and some

A contraband school in Freeman's Village at Arlington, Virginia, across the Potomac River from Washington. *Library of Congress.*

members of the League attended. Early in the evening, the whites, as they came in, took seats on the right side of the room, and the colored people took those on the left, but long before the meeting actually opened the races had intermingled. When speakers announced on the program were delayed in arriving, the colored people became impatient and stamped loudly on the floor until one of them arose to explain that the delay had been caused by a colored man "waiting on a lady who had too many chicken-fixin's to get on." Then the audience sang "My Country 'Tis Of Thee" but the Negroes continued stamping the floor and clapping vigorously until the speakers appeared, after which the meeting progressed peacefully.

About this time, offers of rewards for the capture of fugitive slaves disappeared from the newspapers. Many of Washington's ex-slaves were attending local schools recently established for their special use. Here, according to one visitor, could be seen Negroes from ten to sixty years of age. A gray-haired old Negro was described as "conning his A-B-Cs through his spectacles, and spelling half-aloud with painstaking effort," in the same class with a boy who could have been his grandchild.

On the night of February 10, 1864, there was great excitement at the White House when Lincoln discovered that the stable was on fire. This brick building, described as an "eye-sore," sheltered six horses which could not be removed and were burned to death. Two of them were the property of the Presi-

dent; another pair was owned by John George Nicolay, his private secretary, and the remaining two ponies were those used by Tad, young son of the Lincolns. One of these ponies was more highly prized for it had once belonged to Willie Lincoln, the son who died in 1862. Only three carriages were saved from destruction.

Origin of the fire was a mystery. Early in the evening Mr. Nicolay had given orders to Cooper, the coachman, to have a carriage in readiness at nine o'clock, but the order was countermanded before the coachman left the stable. While Cooper was eating supper, the President, having discovered the smoke, notified him of the fire. Before anyone could reach the stable it was in flames. An alarm was given, and a large crowd was soon on hand to watch steam fire engines being operated by fire fighting companies trying to save the building. The combustible nature of the material inside, and an enormous quantity of old timber scattered nearby, hampered their efforts, and nothing much could be done except to prevent a spread of the flames. The cost of replacing the stables was estimated at twelve thousand dollars.

The coachman lost a trunk containing all his clothing and some gold which he had left in the stable. Colonel L. C. Baker, Provost Marshal of the War Department, was seriously injured by the explosion of a gas pipe, a piece of which struck him in the breast and knocked him senseless. He was revived, but suffered much during the night. Investigations resulted in the conclusion that the fire was the work of an incendiary and suspicion pointed to Patterson McGee, a former coachman of the President who had been discharged the previous day. Since he had been seen at the stable about an hour before the fire was discovered, he was arrested and committed to jail for a hearing early the next morning.

The sole witness examined was a soldier who testified that about dusk, on the night of the fire, he was sitting in a room in the basement of the White House, and saw McGee pass through, but he could not remember exactly the hour this had occurred. McGee had been seen about the stable while it was burning, but said (and it was known to be true) that he had clothing there which he wished to save. He alleged that he was in Grover's Theatre when one of the doorkeepers told him the stable was on fire, and it was only then that he went to the scene. He asked time to send for the doorkeeper, to prove his statement, and it was granted. The presiding justice, however, said that on the testimony he could not further hold McGee. He was released and the origin of the fire remained unsolved.

The following week, Edwin Booth opened a month's engagement at Grover's Theatre in *Hamlet* and other Shakespearean roles. At the Washington Theatre, Laura Keene was appearing in *Our American Cousin*, the play she was to star in again at Ford's Theatre on the night of Lincoln's assassination by Edwin's brother, John. And at Ford's Theatre, during that week of February, 1864, Miss Alice Gray was billed as a favorite young actress playing the part of Alicia in the tragedy of *Jane Shore*. Her photograph was to be found among those of other women on the person of John at the time of his capture and death at Garrett's farm in Virginia.

But the attention and applause given theatrical stars was far surpassed by the ovation to Major General Ulysses S. Grant upon his arrival in the capital. On a late afternoon in March people gathered at the Baltimore and Ohio Railroad depot to get a first glimpse of "the hero of many battles." When the whistle announced the approach of the train, hundreds rushed to the rear of the depot. The General, accompanied by some of his staff, and his son, Fred, alighted from a special car while the crowd cheered and moved along with them. Of moderate build, with a frank, genial face, clear blue eyes, light hair and sandy whiskers mixed with gray, his usual calm and modest appearance seemed somewhat weary from travel.

Inside the depot a company of the Invalid Corps was drawn up in line with arms presented as the General, head uncovered, passed through to the street where hacks waited to take the party to Willard's Hotel. Arriving there, Grant immediately went to the dining-room to be greeted by four hundred guests who arose simultaneously to cheer the war hero. As they pressed toward him, one of the party informed them that the General had traveled some distance, and advised that he should be allowed to consume his "rations" before receiving all who called upon him. He had come to receive the commission of Lieutenant General, and the appointment as General-in-chief of the United States Army, which was formally presented by the President in the presence of the entire Cabinet and high ranking military officers in the Cabinet Chambers. That evening he attended the usual weekly reception at the White House by special invitation of the President, and mounted a crimson-covered sofa to receive an ovation from hundreds of guests in the East Room.

General Grant receiving his commission as Lieutenant-General from President Lincoln, surrounded by the Cabinet and high ranking military officers in the Cabinet chambers. *Library of Congress.*

During his stay in Washington it was announced that he would visit Grover's Theatre with the President and Mrs. Lincoln to see Edwin Booth perform, but other engagements, and his departure, kept him from doing so. At a future date, he was again to disappoint a large audience at Ford's Theatre following a similar notice that he would attend the play, *Our American Cousin*.

Pranks of soldiers, sailors, marines, and rowdy citizens increased, and once again city authorities had trouble in suppressing them. They jammed on the brakes of horsecars, shot at drivers and wounded several; stripped to the waist in public places and fought until someone was knocked out; chased Negroes from their homes, beat policemen with their own clubs, and wrecked government property. One ruffian, who had a whistle similar to those used by the police, stood on a street corner in the red-light district known as "Hooker's Division," and sounded the policeman's call. Police in that neighborhood hastened to the aid of their supposed comrade, but on reaching the corner, he wasn't there. In a few moments the call was sounded at the corner below. Away started the police, but nobody was found at that corner. Finally they got tired trotting through the mud, and, suspecting something wrong, scattered to strategic points and captured the whistler. He was given a night's lodging in jail and fined two dollars before being released.

Not to be outdone, two American Indians staged a gory fight at the United States Hotel. Hole-in-the-Day, chief of the Chippewas, and Look-Around, a young brave of the same tribe, had spent most of the night imbibing liquor. Early the next morning, Look-Around, being drunk, was decorating his headdress with ornaments which Hole-in-the-Day thought "above his grade," and he told Look-Around that he was not yet man enough to wear them. This provoked Look-Around and he fired two shots from a pistol at Hole-in-the-Day. One took effect behind his right ear and, passing around in his head, came out of his mouth. He whipped out a pocket-knife and cut Look-Around across the nose near the forehead and below the gristle. Not until they had grown weak from the loss of blood could they be separated and surgical attention given them. Look-Around was not seriously injured but it was some time before Hole-in-the-Day recovered.

City authorities were again denounced for

A group of Indians in war paint, who visited the White House, were photographed in the conservatory with Mrs. Lincoln (left) and other guests. *National Park Service.*

Hole-in-the-day, Chief of the Chippewas, who fought Look-around to a bloody draw in a Washington hotel. *National Archives.*

THE OLD BULL DOG ON THE RIGHT TRACK.

The Old Bull Dog on the Right Track. *Library of Congress.*

not cleaning Pennsylvania Avenue, and Commissioner B. B. French placed notices in the press reading: "I have only to say that Pennsylvania Avenue is four miles long and one hundred and sixty feet wide, and prior to the establishment of that blessing to all citizens, the horse railroad, was pretty much cut to pieces by omnibuses; and the work of injury has since been nearly completed by army wagons. To keep *all this road* in repair, Congress appropriated last year six thousand dollars. I called the attention of Congress to the condition of the Avenue in my last report, and to the inadequacy of the appropriation, and asked for *twenty thousand dollars*, which sum, judiciously expended, might keep the Avenue in decent order."

Policemen, too, decided they were being pushed around for too little pay and held a meeting at the Council chambers. They contended that the price of living in Washington had increased at least one hundred percent, particularly in house rent and necessary provisions, and that no policeman, although exer-

cising the most prudent economy, could make the scanty pittance received support himself and family. Hence, at the expiration of the month, he found himself in debt for the actual necessities of life. They called attention to the very responsible duties devolving on District policemen, requiring more than usual vigilance, skill, and business tact, and that to secure efficient and honest men, they must be placed above want and temptation. After much deliberation they agreed to ask for, and got, a salary increase of seventy-five dollars per month.

Buffed by war news good and bad, bewildered, crestfallen, or joyful, the people of Washington still hoped, prayed, and celebrated each time the slaughter seemed to be near the end. Now they were to read that a considerable portion of the Army of the Potomac had changed its position in Virginia so materially that at any moment they might hear of the most extensive and important battle of the war. "The change of position was made," the report said, "without any demon-

Andrew Johnson, a Tennessee tailor who rose to political fame as a staunch defender of the Union. *National Archives.*

stration that it was going on; not an additional tap of a drum, or blast of bugle was permitted, and no stragglers bringing up the rear as in

our energies to that point. Now, without detaining you any longer, I propose that you help me to close what I am now saying with

poses to throw the weight of his army first on Smith hoping to crush him before Grant can reach within co-operative distance of Smith. The belief is that Lee means to confront Grant directly, therefore these changes with this purpose in view. It is certain from Grant's past history that his movements will be rapid and telling."

Within a few days, newspaper columns headed EXTRA reported: "Stirring News From The Front; Movements Of Lee And Grant; Fighting Going On Near The Wilderness; Attack Upon Petersburg; Our Army In Full Pursuit Of The Enemy Towards Richmond." Such joyful tidings prompted gatherings of residents in public places, and serenades to various Government officials. Lincoln's renomination at Baltimore for the presidency drew another large crowd to the grounds of the White House where, after a band had played "Hail To The Chief" and "The Soldiers Chorus," he appeared upon the steps of the main entrance and answered their shouts for a speech with these words:

"Gentlemen: I am very much obliged to you for this compliment. I have just been saying, and as I have just said it, I will repeat it —the hardest of all speeches which I have to answer is a serenade. I never know what to say on such occasions. I suppose that you have done me this kindness in connection with the action of the Baltimore convention, which has recently taken place, and with which, of course, I am very well satisfied. (Laughter and applause.) What we want still more than Baltimore conventions or presidential elections is success under General Grant. (Cries of 'Good' and applause.) I suppose that you constantly bear in mind that the support you owe to the brave officers and soldiers in the field is of the very first importance, and we should, therefore, bend all

son, a Tennessee tailor who had risen to political fame as a staunch defender of the Union. But as the days passed, the good news of Union victories soured and the hope of an immediate end to the war began to fade once again.

Late June, and the siege of Petersburg was on full blast. "FROM GRANT'S ARMY," roared the presses while guns thundered as if in unison. "The Unsuccessful Assaults. Our Losses During The Past Ten Days 8,000 Killed. Captured 1,200 Prisoners." Day after day, week after week, month after month, the news from Grant came in: "Rebels Gain A Temporary Success But Are Finally Repulsed. All Railroads Leading Into Richmond Destroyed." July: "GRANT'S MINE AT PETERSBURG EXPLODED: Rebels designed to damage a mine they suspected of being dug. An explosion, or whatever it was, startled our men. Everyone rushed to his post when rapid fire commenced from our line in direction of enemy supposed to be advancing. When the smoke cleared, the mistake was discovered." August: "LATEST FROM GRANT'S ARMY: Terrific Explosion At City Point. Two Barges Loaded With Ordnance Stores Blows Up. Fearful Loss Of Life. Between Two And Three Hundred Persons Killed Or Wounded. Twenty-seven Sacks Of Heads, Arms, And Legs Picked Up On The Shore." Again that month: "Desperate Rebel Attacks On Our Works In Front Of Petersburg." September: "NO FURTHER MOVEMENTS AT PETERSBURG."

Reports that Atlanta had been captured echoed like a cry from the wilderness as every means of transportation brought Grant's wounded soldiers into Washington. In one day 150 deserters (skedaddlers) from his army arrived by boat and were turned over to the Provost Marshal's office. A captain, with swollen feet, claiming to have been

Punishment in the Army turned soldiers into acrobats. *Library of Congress.*

struck by a shell, was reported by the examining surgeon to have been "disabled from running off the battlefield."

During the summer, a violent explosion and fire at the Arsenal was one of the city's worse catastrophes. While more than 'one hundred girls were making cartridges in the main laboratory, a quantity of fireworks outside of the building became ignited, and a piece of fuse blew into the room where many of them were working. The explosion which followed raised the roof and set fire to the building. This started a panic, and the girls jumped from windows or rushed through doorways as the flames spread. News of the frightful explosion and fire brought a large crowd to the Arsenal, but not even relatives of the girls were allowed to enter the grounds for the fire was rapidly destroying the entire building.

"A singular feature of the sad spectacle," it was reported, "was that presented by a number of the bodies nearly burned to a cinder being caged, as it were, in the wire of their hooped skirts. These bodies seemed more badly burned than those not thus enveloped in hoops, and it is probable that the expansion of the dress by the hoops afforded

142

facilities for the flames to fasten upon them with fatal effect. We would suggest, in this connection, that operatives working in such dangerous localities, should by all means wear non-combustive clothing. Cloth washed in alum water is said to be fire-proof." Homage to those fatally burned was paid by all of Washington at a special funeral service in their honor. Many people also accompanied the funeral procession as it moved along Pennsylvania Avenue to the Congressional Burying Ground.

The United States arsenal was located on the present site of the Army War College. Its foundries, work-shops, magazines, and laboratories, contained everything necessary for the manufacture of implements and materials of war. *National Archives.*

Washington Evening Star.

That summer an investigation of alleged dishonesty in the Treasury Department revealed an unexpected scandal. It was reported that the Director of Printing had converted his bureau into a place of drinking and debauchery, employing only young and beautiful girls who would submit to his wishes. The father of one testified under oath that his daughter had been promised a raise in salary of seventy-five dollars a month if she would yield to the Director's desires. The father did not elaborate, but the investigation placed a stigma on every female employee of the Treasury Department.

A good way for fathers of families to aid recruiting.
Library of Congress.

A number of persons in the District, in anticipation of another draft, had been hunting substitutes, and the trade in them was becoming very brisk. The officer of the Provost Marshal office, besides examining the applications for exemption, had been kept busy in examining persons offered as substitutes, most of whom were contrabands from Virginia, and were not subject to the draft. The price paid was between $250 and $500. The proclamation by the President called for a draft throughout the United States for 500,000 men of whom 4,256 were to come from the District. Before these soldiers were drafted, however, Confederate General Jubal Early's army of veterans gave Washington, and Lincoln too, a closer view of the war.

Local items in the press of July 2, 1864, reported that the President and his family would occupy their rooms at the Old Soldiers' Home that afternoon for the first time that season. It was located just off the Seventh Street Road on the outskirts of Washington, and not far from Fort Stevens. During his journeys to and from "his summer resort" the Union Light Guard (Ohio Cavalry) consisting of twenty men acted as his body guard, "escorting him from the White House in the evening to the Soldiers' Home, and returning again in the morning."

Following the national holiday, reports of Confederate raids into Maryland and the capture of a considerable amount of supplies filled the newspapers. Day after day the reports grew more alarming; it was apparent the rebel advance was toward Washington. Union forces at Harper's Ferry had fought spiritedly but were outmaneuvered in every direction. Nearby Frederick, Maryland, was in the hands of rebel raiders—15,000 strong. They continued to push forward. "EXTRA! EXTRA! THE INVASION!" read boldfaced type. "REBELS APPEAR AT ROCKVILLE IN SOME FORCE!" It was now evident they were headed for Fort Stevens, on Seventh Street Road just north of the capital.

Evening Star.

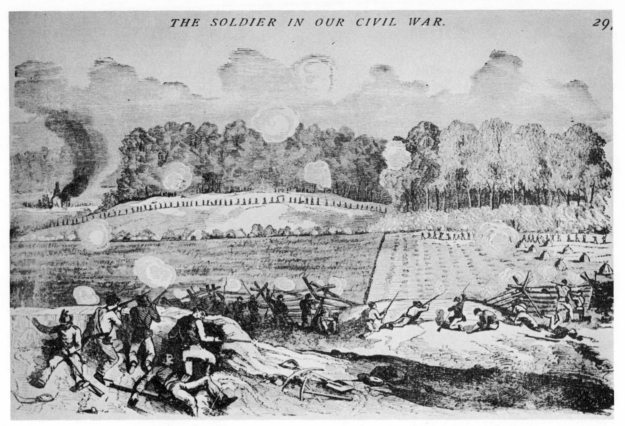

Confederate assault by troops of General Jubal Early on Fort Stevens near Washington, July 11, 1864. *National Park Service.*

Rebel attack continued throughout the night and was observed by Lincoln on horseback (left). Tall chimneys (center) were all that was left of the Francis P. Blair home destroyed during the battle. *Library of Congress.*

SCENES NEAR WASHINGTON, DURING THE REBEL RAID—NIGHT ATTACK, JULY 11, ON FORT STEVENS WHILE THE PRESIDENT WAS THERE.

Newspapers of July 12 brought on more excitement: "EXTRA! EXTRA!" they blazed, "The Condition Of Things Last Night—The Fighting Out On The Seventh Street Road—Rebel Sharpshooters Dislodged—The Enemy Attempted To Plant A Battery But Are Shelled Away—Policemen And Other Citizens Take A Hand In The Fighting!" Following the headlines came the report that "The heavy skirmishing in front of Fort Stevens, in the vicinity of Seventh Street Road yesterday afternoon, continued until after dark. Confederate forces moved to a position in the woods; they fired from behind trees and crept along the road until they succeeeded in getting within range of the Fort. They used no artillery but sharpshooters picked off our gunners. At 6:30 P.M. our cavalry charged and threw the rebels back some distance. At 7 P.M. the infantry was brought up and placed in line in front of Fort Stevens while our cavalry deployed at the right. The District Militia has been called out."

Skirmishing in front of the fort had been suspended by a heavy rain about 2 P.M. that day, the heaviest fighting having been between 5 and 7 P.M. "A number of our soldiers were overcome by the heat, as were also several citizens who had walked out to the scene of action to witness the engagement," read this report. "Early in the evening thousands of persons could be seen passing out Seventh Street by every conceivable means of conveyance, while the road was literally lined with pedestrians. The hills, trees and fences within sight of Fort Stevens were covered with human beings, quite a number of whom were ladies. Quietly seated in a carriage, at a commanding point, was Secretary Seward, viewing the progress of affairs." It was also while viewing the progress of affairs that Lincoln, standing on a parapet of Fort Stevens, was a target for enemy bullets. According to an eye-witness: "A medical officer standing beside him threw up his hands and collapsed. A minnie ball from a sharpshooter had cut him down. General [Horatio G.] Wright, in command of the fort, ran up and dragged the President of the United States right down off that parapet."

News on the following day (July 13) brought relief to the city's population: "THE

Standing on a parapet next day (July 12) Lincoln saw a Union medical officer shot down within a few feet of him by a rebel sharpshooter. No time was lost in getting the President off the elevation. *National Park Service.*

REBELS HAVE DISAPPEARED FROM OUR FRONT. Believed To Be In Full Retreat Across The Potomac. They Leave Their Dead And Wounded Behind Them." In this same issue another report read: "President Lincoln and Mrs. Lincoln passed along the line of the city defense in a carriage last night, and were warmly greeted by the soldiers wherever they made their appearance amongst them. The night was beautiful, a peaceful moonlight, and a large proportion of the population of the city was out to a late hour, waiting in anticipation that the rebels might make some demonstration in pursuance of their old tactics of night attacks. Considerable attention was attracted by the signaling going on between the different stations at the Soldiers' Home, 18th Street and elsewhere, and especially the brilliant lights displayed from the tower at the Soldiers' Home, seen for a long distance."

With the rebels on the run, at least in a direction other than Washington, another Great War Meeting was held in the capital. It was described as a large and enthusiastic gathering, voicing a resolution to thoroughly prosecute the war. In compliance with the earnest request of the crowd, the President made a few remarks expressing the same determination.

In September, Mr. Thomas Burns, "the well-known blind man" who had drawn the names from the bowl during a previous draft, was again on hand to perform his duties. Negroes also took an active part in helping to raise funds or men to fill the District quota. At a meeting held for that purpose, one of them said that old colored men would not have to fight, but the young ones would, and they should come forward and contribute liberally. He wanted to save these young men if he could, but their money was the only thing that would do it. By buying substitutes they did not rob the battlefields, and if a certain fund was raised they would be clear for a little while at least. Another said that he was an old man, not subject to the draft, and he would not give a "damn cent" to save his own son or anyone else from it, for it was the colored man's golden opportunity to fight

for his own freedom. Those of their race had greater reason to fight than any class of men in the world, he declared, and they ought to prove themselves worthy of the freedom they enjoyed. Slavery was their greatest enemy and they must fight it down.

Lincoln, meanwhile, wishing to have his own substitute in the army (who would be credited to the Third Ward in which the President lived), selected John Summerfield Staples of Pennsylvania. Eighteen years of age, not quite as tall as the President, but strong and healthy, he had seen service in a militia regiment and had fulfilled all the requirements of a fine soldier. After his father had consented to his enlistment, the bounty paid by Lincoln was handed over to the recruit. Two days later, young Staples, in the uniform of the Union army, and accompanied by his father, Provost Marshal General James B. Fry, and others, was received by the President at the White House. General Fry introduced the new recruit by saying: "Mr. President, this is the man who is to represent you in the army for the next year." Lincoln shook hands with the soldier and said that such an honest-looking young man could be relied upon to do his duty. The President was then presented with a framed official notice of the fact that he had put a representative recruit into the military service of the United States Army. As the party turned to leave, Lincoln again shook hands with the soldier, and expressed the hope that he would be "one of the fortunate ones." To a certain extent he was, for years later, when he applied for a pension, his disabilities were not of a serious nature.

That same month (October 1864) Ford's New Theatre announced the first appearance of Junius Brutus Booth, Jr., since his return from California after an absence of twelve years. He opened in *Richard III*, and in the cast were: E. A. Emerson, Jennie Gourlay, Mrs. E. Muzzy, H. B. Phillips, and Alice Gray, all of whom were to perform in a play on the night Booth's brother John Wilkes assassinated Lincoln in that same theatre. Of the Booths, a Washington newspaper had this to say: "Three, at least, of the four sons of the late. J. B. Booth, the tragedian, appear to have inherited the brilliant genius of their renowned father. Two of these—Edwin and John Wilkes —are already known to the play-going public in Washington, and the third, and not least gifted—Junius Brutus, eldest of the three brothers—will, through the enterprise of Mr. Ford, be introduced to our public at Ford's Theatre next Monday night. Mr. Booth has but recently returned from California, where, in the past fifteen years, he has been gathering up the richest of 'golden opinions.' He is a brilliant actor, of the nervous and intellectual school, is liberally endowed with the best physical requirements of his profession, and remarkably resembles his father in the earlier days of the latter."

His engagement had not yet terminated on the evening of the great torch light political procession sponsored by the Lincoln and Johnson Clubs in the city. Members and friends marched along streets carrying all sorts of blazing devices favoring election of Republican candidates. Howitzers boomed, bands played, crowds cheered, and rockets were sent up from the roof of the Patent Of-fice building. The procession was about forty minutes in passing a given point, and when spread out it resembled a myriad of glimmering stars. At all places where the clubs' flags were displayed, men in the line of march shouted their approval, but the sight of a McClellan flag (the opposition emblem) made them groan as if in agony. Bands, on approaching the flags in front of Parker's Hall (meeting place of the Democrats), stopped all music and walked under them in silence. Several soldiers, in passing, remarked that they had once admired McClellan, but now had little regard for him as the Democratic nominee for the presidency.

The procession then marched to the White House where many people had gathered. A continual illumination was kept up by the display of fireworks, and the President was recognized at an upper window with his son, Tad. Answering loud and repeated calls for a speech, he said: "Fellow-citizens: I was promised not to be called upon for a speech tonight, nor do I propose to make one. But, as we have been hearing some very good news for a day or two, I propose that you give

A cartoon depicting Lincoln as being amused over the candidness of "Little Mac" (McClellan) his opponent of the Democratic ticket. *National Park Service.*

Reception at the War Department, October 29, 1864, of guns captured from the enemy by General Phil Sheridan. *Washington Public Library.*

three hearty cheers for [General Philip] Sheridan [who had turned defeat into victory at Cedar Creek]. I propose three cheers for General Grant, who knew what use to put Sheridan; three cheers for all our noble commanders and the soldiers and sailors; three cheers for all the people everywhere who cheer the soldiers and sailors of the Union—and now, goodnight." At this time, guns captured by Sheridan were on view in the grounds fronting the War Department building.

Some fighting, the burning of a McClellan flag, and several arrests, enlivened the evening. In view of the immense number of persons on the streets, the amount of cannon-firing, and the incessant discharge of fireworks, it was remarkable that nothing of a more serious nature occurred.

Nearly 50,000 people left Washington homeward bound to vote in the presidential election that November. At times the rush to board trains was so great that extra railroad guards had to be called into action, principally because soldiers, in their anxiety to get away, threatened to tear down the railing at the gate and attempt to board cars by climbing through the windows. At the Armory Square Hospital soldiers, after signing the roll for their paychecks, had written down the name of the candidate they preferred for the presidency. The results were: Lincoln, 260; McClellan, 116; Fremont, 3; total 379; Lincoln's majority, 141.

On election night rain, fog, and muddy streets failed to keep residents indoors. Almost before the street gaslights were turned on, people with umbrellas and rolled-up trousers began to roam about in quest of news. As early returns began to come in, the bobbing of umbrellas above the heads of those on their way to club rooms and hotels caused one reporter to observe that "the rain and umbrellas averted many a row, for no man can fight well holding a spread umbrella, and by the time he shuts it and loops it up, his angry passions have had time to simmer down, especially if it is raining pretty hard."

The main rallying points that night were the Republican quarters at the Union League and the Democratic Association rooms at Parker's Hall. Returns from various parts of the country kept the Republicans cheering and there were loud calls for speeches. Congratulating the crowd on the "glorious news coming in," one politician remarked that the result of the election would be "painful for Jeff Davis and his tribe." He mentioned the name of Buchanan and some one cried, "The damn Copperhead!" Then "the Hallelujah song was sung with a vim."

Cheering at Parker's Hall was spasmodic. The New York and Baltimore city returns, reported as favoring McClellan, were wildly greeted but dispatches numbering the elec-

toral votes for Lincoln were received in grim silence. One Democrat urged those present to put no confidence in such dispatches for they came from Republican sources, but dozens of persons left the room saying "the jig is up." At the door, however, some one cried "fight" and several hundred Democrats rushed down the stairs shouting "Rally, McClellan men! Democrats to the rescue!" Upon reaching the street the crowd pushed its way into the Metropolitan Hotel, cheering for their Democratic candidates. A scuffle began between a number of the opposing parties and a few persons were knocked down. Police arrived, broke up the fight, and the McClellan men returned to Parker's Hall where a burly fellow announced in a loud voice that a fight was going on at the Union League, and suggested that all Democrats "fall in and go up there to see it out." Another Democratic managed to quiet the crowd and all contented themselves by again cheering for McClellan. Gradually the throng in the hall thinned to about three hundred who remained for some time hoping to hear better news.

Hotels were beginning to fill up again with returned office-seekers, lobbyists, and contract-wranglers. Mrs. Lincoln, knowing

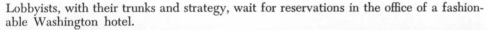

Lobbyists, with their trunks and strategy, wait for reservations in the office of a fashionable Washington hotel.

the President would have little to do with any of them, had dealt with the lobbyists herself, using their flattery and offering of bribes to advantage. One newspaper reported her as saying of the lobbyists: "I have an object in view. In a political canvass, it is policy to cultivate every element of strength. These men have influence and we require influence to elect Mr. Lincoln. I will be clever with them until after the election, and then, if we remain at the White House, I will drop every one of them, and let them know very plainly that I only made tools of them. They are an unprincipled set, and I don't mind a little double dealing with them."

As returns began to indicate Lincoln's re-election, enthusiastic Republicans marched through the streets singing "Rally Round The Flag, Boys, Rally Once Again." For hours they kept up a continual din in downtown

Contractors are back, spreading cheer everywhere.

Rally Round The Flag, Boys! Rally Once Again! *Library of Congress.*

Washington which reached a climax about half-past one o'clock in the morning of November 9 when some of them serenaded Lincoln at the White House. Appearing at one of the windows, the President said in part: "I am thankful to God for this approval of the people; but, while deeply gratified for this mark of their confidence in me, if I know my heart, my gratitude is free from any taint of personal triumph. I do not impugn the motives of anyone opposed to me. It is no pleasure to me to triumph over anyone. But I give thanks to the Almighty for this evidence of the people's resolution to stand by free government and the rights of humanity."

What Lincoln said about the motives of anyone opposed to him was little consolation for Edward Green. He had lost an election wager and at dawn that morning began sawing a cord of pine wood in the street opposite the Post Office. All day long he sawed and people stopped to watch and wag him on. He seemed to have had no previous experience with a saw and often paused to pant and regain his breath. Although his progress was slow, by sundown he had finished the job and paid his debt.

In the wake of the election, visitors to the White House stole and destroyed furnishings in their eagerness to get relics of their sight-seeing sprees. Wantonly they snipped pieces from window curtains, sofa, lounge and chair covers, and went so far as to pull the papering from walls, remove heavy brackets from windows, and tassels from curtains. The hangings in the East Room and Green Room were badly cut up, and nineteen out of twenty brackets from the windows of the East Room were stolen. Three ladies, whose names were not known, were "caught in the act" and one fainted.

But an elk-horn chair, which had just been

Lincoln examining the rifle of Seth Kinman after the California hunter had presented him with an elkhorn chair. *Library of Congress.*

given to Lincoln, managed to escape the souvenir hunters. It was the handiwork of Seth Kinman, a woodsman of renown from California, who had come to Washington for the presentation ceremony. The press described him as dressed in a full suit of buckskin: pants, heavy coat, and a large fur hat, which, with his flowing beard, gave him a unique appearance. He had attracted much attention on Pennsylvania Avenue, and at Ford's Theatre which he had attended the evening before calling on the President. "He carries his rifle with him on all occasions and delights in having his picture taken," read one newspaper report.

The article stated that the President had greeted him pleasantly and, after examining the chair "minutely," sat in it and expressed himself as highly pleased with the workmanship. It was made almost entirely of elk horns, firmly braced together, the seat made of elk skin with the hair on it and highly ornamented. Mr. Kinman told the President that it had taken him about seven years to collect the material from which the chair was made, and that the rifle which had killed the elks

155

Rally of the troops at Washington. *National Archives.*

also had killed the British General Packenham at New Orleans in 1815. Later it was carried through the Black Hawk war by his father who had served in the company with Lincoln at that time.

He then informed the President that he had another little keepsake with him in the form of a fiddle made from the skull of his favorite mule, which, when alive, appeared to have music in his soul, for he would always look around the camps on the plains when he heard music. After the mule had been dead for some time, he passed his bleached bones one day and the idea struck him that there might be music in the bones, so he made the fiddle. Later he took a rib, and some hairs from the tail, and made the bow. Much to the amusement of Lincoln and other spectators, he played "Essence of Old Virginia" and "John Brown" on the bones of the mule. Lincoln said that if he could play a fiddle he would ask him for it, but since he could not, the fiddle would be better off in Mr. Kinman's hands.

News of General William T. Sherman's steady advance through Georgia was now the topic in Washington. Early in December, Lincoln had described Sherman's attempted march of three hundred miles directly through the insurgent region as the most remarkable feature in the military operations of the year.

"It tends to show," he said, "a great increase in our relative strength that our General-in-Chief should feel able to confront and hold in check every active force of the enemy, and yet detail a well appointed large army to move on such an expedition. The result not yet being known, conjecture in regard to it is not here indulged."

With each newspaper account of the Union army's progress, Washington residents grew more and more excited. Reports came in as thick and fast as the salvos of Sherman's guns in the deep South: "JOYFUL NEWS FROM SHERMAN. Only Ten Miles From Savannah. March Unchecked. Our Success Thus Far Perfect." At eight o'clock on the morning of December 26 a salute of three hundred guns was fired in Franklin Square to celebrate the dispatch Lincoln had received the previous night which read:

Savannah, Georgia, December 22, 1864

To His Excellency President Lincoln:
I beg to present you, as a Christmas gift, the city of Savannah, with one hundred and fifty heavy guns and plenty of ammunition; and also about twenty-five thousand (25,000) bales of cotton.

W. T. Sherman, Major General

For the Union, 1864 had been a good year.

Shadows in the Streets

Lincoln's last New Year's reception followed the familiar pattern of previous affairs on that date. Customary precautions were taken to protect the carpets, and, after high ranking officials had arrived and departed, the gates to the grounds were thrown open, and the crowd rushed into the White House.

"At half-past two the jam was terrific," one report read, "and many pressed so determinedly to gain admittance that several ladies and children were raised above the crowd by their male protectors in order to shield them from pressure. One lady reached the door in such a dilapidated condition (her bonnet be-

Samuel Arnold. *Library of Congress.*

Michael O'Loughlin. *Library of Congress.*

ing mashed and her shawl torn nearly in twain) that she said she would not go into the presence of Mr. Lincoln in that condition, and inquired the nearest way out. One man, who was determined to see the President, come what might, had the tail of his long cloak well fastened between four or five

Lewis Payne. *Library of Congress.*

men in the rear, and concluding to leave the garment behind, unlooped it from his neck, and made his way in. The police did their best to prevent crowding, but the pressure was too much for them."

During the previous year, John Wilkes Booth's stage career, and an annual income of some twenty thousand dollars, had been threatened by prolonged bronchitis, his oil investments in Pennsylvania had dwindled to nothing, and fame and fortune seemed to be departing from him. How could he, with one bold stroke, regain his prestige in the South where audiences had applauded his theatrical performances, and beautiful women had swooned in his arms? The plan he was formulating must be worked out in secret, yet it required help from others. Who would act as he directed? Whom could he trust? How many would be needed for so dangerous a venture? Where could he find them? In trying to answer these questions effectively, he rounded up an amazing group of accomplices.

On trips to Baltimore, Booth had met Samuel Bland Arnold, Michael O'Laughlin, and Lewis Payne. He had known them before; Arnold and O'Laughlin had been his boyhood friends, and all three men had served in the Confederate army. Arnold, who had a rather stern face, dark hair and moustache, had deserted the rebel forces and worked as a clerk and farm laborer. O'Laughlin, also a deserter, resembled Booth, with the exception that he wore a tuft of hair on his chin known as an "imperial." Payne, tall and husky, with heavy-set jaws, scowling eyes, and a shock of black hair dangling over a low forehead, had been captured at Gettysburg, then deserted the rebel cause rather than be exchanged as a prisoner.

John Surratt. *National Park Service.*

David E. Herold. *National Park Service.*

While in Washington and Southern Maryland, Booth had met David E. Herold, John Harrison Surratt, George Atzerodt, and Dr. Samuel Mudd, rebel stooges and sympathizers. Herold, a slender youth with small, weak eyes and a stolid face bearing an immature growth of hair, was foolhardy and undependable. He lived with several sisters near the Navy Yard and had worked as an apothecary's clerk in a Washington drugstore. Surratt, tall and slender, with a prominent forehead, large nose, sunken eyes, a goatee, and long light-colored hair, was a rebel spy and dispatch carrier, a connecting link in the underground between Richmond and the

Confederate "Little Cabinet" in Canada. Atzerodt, stubby, round-shouldered, with ill-kept brown hair, goatee, sickly-looking skin, and dull-witted face, aided the rebels in crossing the Potomac in lower Maryland. By trade, he was a carriage-maker. Dr. Samuel Mudd, the most intelligent of the group, was a tall, slender man with a long narrow face, small piercing eyes and a high forehead.

All had been drawn into a plan Booth had concocted to make himself a hero of the Confederacy. They were to abduct Lincoln and carry him off to Richmond to be held as hostage for the return of rebel prisoners, or, perhaps, to end the war on terms of the Con-

George A. Atzerodt. *National Park Service.*

Dr. Samuel Mudd. *National Park Service.*

Mrs. Mary Surratt. *National Park Service.*

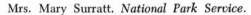

federacy. Some of them frequented the boarding house of Mrs. Mary Surratt on H Street, Northwest. Her firm lips, steadfast eyes, and dark hair parted in the middle and combed flat around a large forehead, gave her an uncompromising appearance. She was a widow and mother of John, Anna, and Isaac, the latter son having enlisted in the Confederate army. Mrs. Surratt had reason to be interested in the abduction scheme but it is doubtful that she had knowledge of any other plot against the President.

The first effort to abduct Lincoln, according to later evidence, was planned for a night in January 1865, when he expected to be at

Ford's Theatre during the engagement of Edwin Forrest, America's greatest tragedian. Lincoln attended several performances, but failed to show up on the date selected by the conspirators to carry him off to Richmond. The announcement that John Sleeper Clarke, popular comedian, would appear at Ford's Theatre in a round of his most celebrated characters, was welcomed as a relief from the heavy plays which Forrest had presented there. The brother-in-law of the Booths was gaining an enviable reputation on the stage, which was to be shattered within a short time. During his engagement, the President and General Grant, who was in the capital with his family, attended the theatre. Wilkes Booth, then in New York visiting Edwin, was still bent upon pursuing his mad course, prompted by his hatred of Lincoln and the Union.

By March, preparations for Lincoln's second inauguration and the inaugural ball were in full swing. The press announced that it had been authorized by the committee to say there was no truth in the story which had been circulated that tickets to the ball had been sold to Negroes. Andrew Johnson, Vice President-elect, had arrived and crowds again were gathering in the capital. General McClellan, whom Lincoln had defeated for President, was in Europe for a protracted vacation and Parker's Hall (headquarters of the Democrats) was quiet. Among the hundreds of people attending the closing session of Congress were Wilkes Booth and John Surratt. Booth was reported to have said that the booming of guns in forts surrounding Washington was driving him crazy. But it could not have been more than routine practice that upset him, such as that at the Navy Yard on Eastern Point, less than a mile from the Capitol.

The Washington Navy Yard (with shad fishers in the foreground) was located on the eastern branch of the Potomac River about three-quarters of a mile from the capital. Two large ship houses flank the main building of offices and shops with the unfinished dome of the Capitol looming up in the rear. *Library of Congress.*

Crowd attending Lincoln's second inauguration. *National Park Service.*

The day of the inauguration was ushered in by a night of drizzling rain. During the early morning a gale swept the city, uprooting trees and causing other damages. Streets were filled with mud (described as "black plaster") which defied both horses and men to pass through it. It was a dreary outlook for those who were to take part in the procession and did not relish having their "fancy fixin's spoiled by water and mudbath combined." The Engineer Corps surveyed and took sound-ings of the Avenue to determine the practicability of laying pontoons from the Capitol to the White House, but found the bottom too soft to hold the anchors of the boats, and the project was abandoned. Police were careful to confine to the sidewalks all persons "who could not swim." Nevertheless, at shallow crossings, where steady streams of people passed throughout the day, some dashed out into the Avenue in a most reckless manner. Fortunately no one was injured.

Lincoln delivers his second inaugural address while John Wilkes Booth, probably among those at upper right, and Lewis Payne, believed to be standing directly below the President and wearing a large light-colored hat, hear him say: "with malice toward none: with charity for all. . . ." *National Park Service.*

Rumors that day did not include the fact that Wilkes Booth again was stalking about the city, his mind still intent upon some foul blow to the President. They did spread the idea, however, that "something was going on" —that trouble was anticipated from some undeveloped quarter. There also were rumors that all the roads leading into Washington were heavily picketed, and that soldiers were guarding bridges with extra vigilance as if in watch for suspicious characters; that the Eighth Illinois Cavalry had been sent from Fairfax Courthouse on an active scouting expedition, apparently in search of them, and that the unusual number of "ornry-looking cusses" in shabby clothes seen upon the streets indicated trouble. The fact that military patrols had been doubled and were making more frequent rounds of the streets added to the excitement, but only pickpockets and rowdies were tracked down and the inaugural ceremonies were held as scheduled.

A platform had been erected on the steps of the east front of the Capitol to accommodate the President and his suite, and all entrances to the building were closed except to those having coveted cards of admission. "The old trick of shysters, 'Members of the press, sir,' did not work at all," according to one report. "The precautions against all such schemes were well taken and nonplussed many a complacent chap who flattered himself with the idea of his own peculiar cuteness. The Sergeant-at-arms was courteous but inexorable. The regular representatives of the press belonging to Congress received tickets promptly; to all others an invariable refusal was given."

Many, however, availed themselves of senatorial influence to secure passes, and not a few slipped in several hours previous to the ceremonies. Wilkes Booth, having received a pass from former Senator John P. Hale of New Hampshire, was in the crowd. "I was so close to the President that I could have shot him, had I wanted to," he later confided to a friend.

At this second inauguration, Lincoln spoke the famous words:

"With malice toward none; with charity for all, with firmness in the right, as God gives us to see the right, let us strive on to finish the work we are in; to bind up the nation's wounds; to care for him who shall have borne the battle, and for his widow, and his orphan, to do all which may achieve and cherish a just and a lasting peace among ourselves, and with all the nations."

After the inaugural procession was dismissed, and participants had gone to their quarters to get the mud off their clothing, the Superintendent of Police and the sergeants made preparations for the night. They strengthened the force in thickly populated precincts which might be disturbed by intemperance, but despite the gayety displayed throughout Washington, it was the most orderly night that had succeeded an inauguration since the first term of Andrew Jackson.

Few drunken men were seen staggering about the streets; no assaults, robberies, or riots occurred, and newspaper reports of other offenses were of little importance. The police and soldiers assigned to keep order at the White House reception, nevertheless, were extremely busy. Described by one reporter, the scene was almost identical to that of the New Year gatherings:

"At eight o'clock the gates were thrown open, when the grand rush was made by at least two thousand persons to gain entrance to the building, and the hustling and jolting was terrific. Some of the more unfortunate females who were caught in the surging mass, actually shrieked in pain, while several fainted and were carried away. It was impossible to let all into the Mansion at once, but at each opening of the doors the same scenes were renewed, and after parties did get into the vestibule, some of them presented a doleful appearance indeed, with dresses or coats a good deal the worse for the mess."

The President, wearing his usual plain black

Salmon P. Chase, Chief Justice of the United States, administers the oath of office to the re-elected President. *National Park Service.*

Drawing of Lincoln's last reception in the White House and "key" to the notables who were there. *National Park Service.*

suit and white kid gloves, seemed in excellent spirits notwithstanding the fatiguing ordeals through which he had passed during the day. It was estimated that he shook hands with some six thousand individuals that evening. One was young John Burroughs, the Treasury Department clerk, who had memorized "a little speech" he expected to repeat at the proper moment, but Lincoln "just drew him along, dropping his hand to take the next one in line." Relating the incident later in life, Burroughs, then a famous naturalist, added, "How green I was; yes, how green I was."

Many came as late as eleven o'clock, and at times the walks from the Avenue to the White House were completely blocked. The reception closed before all succeeded in getting in, and the late arrivals were compelled to return

1. Senator Anthony. 2. Senator Fessenden. 3. Major-Gen. Foster. 4. Major-Gen. Sherman. 5. Hon. E. G. Squier. 6. Mrs. Stephens. 7. Senator Sumner. 8. Major-Gen. Kilpatrick. 9. Major-Gen. Banks. 10. Mrs. E. G. Squier. 11. Major-Gen. Sheridan. 12. Major-Gen. Hancock. 13. Admiral Farragut. 14. Governor Curtin. 15. Major-Gen. Logan. 16. Major-Gen. Hooker. 17. Hon. Horace Greeley. 18. Lieut.-Gen. Grant. 19. Major-Gen. Butler. 20. Hon. H. J. Raymond. 21. Admiral Porter. 22. Mrs. Gen. Grant. 23. President Johnson. 24. Major-Gen. Howard. 25. The late President Lincoln. 26. Major-Gen. Dix. 27. Mrs. Lincoln. 28. Chief Justice Chase. 29. Secretary Stanton. 30. Hon. Cassius C. Clay. 31. Mrs. Senator Sprague. 32. Major-Gen. Slocum. 33. Secretary Seward. 34. Speaker Colfax. 35. Mrs. Douglas. 36. Secretary Welles. 37. Mr. J. G. Bennett.

home without paying their respects to the President and Mrs. Lincoln.

The Sunday following the inauguration was pleasant and cheerful, and downtown streets were thronged with strangers. Residents were lost in the crowd of visitors moving to and from various places of interest, and neighbors looked in vain for the face of an acquaintance. It being the first sabbath in March, communion services were held in many churches. Congregations were large and included an unusual number of clergymen of different denominations representing most sections of the country. Some of them had been cut off from contact with their brethren north of Virginia since 1860.

The President, Mrs. Lincoln, Secretary Stanton, Chief Justice Salmon P. Chase, Admiral David G. Farragut, and many others equally distinguished, attended religious services in the Capitol by Bishop Matthew Simpson of the Methodist Church. Within two months the Bishop was to conduct the burial ceremonies at Lincoln's funeral in Springfield, Illinois.

Next evening, the Inaugural Ball attracted an estimated four thousand people who became quite boisterous before the night ended. The spacious rooms of the Patent Office were gaily decorated and gas jets flared above the throng of notables and the social elite of the city. According to one observer: "The dress display was rich and varied, New York belle-dom taking the lead in this department, though Washington (perhaps dividing honors with Philadelphia) carried off the palm for beauty."

Three bands were provided: Wither's Band for the dancing, Lillie's Finley Hospital Band for the promenade music, and the Band of the Ninth Veteran Reserve Corps for the supper rooms. Dancing began shortly before ten o'clock, but within an hour it was interrupted by the strains of "Hail To The Chief," announcing the arrival of the Presidential party. Lincoln was accompanied by Speaker Schuyler Colfax, and Mrs. Lincoln was escorted by Senator Charles Sumner of Massachusetts.

Mrs. Lincoln's white silk dress was trimmed with a bertha of point lace and puffs of silk. She wore a necklace, a bracelet, and earrings of pearls, and carried a white fan trimmed with ermine and silver spangles, white kid gloves and a lace handkerchief. Her hair was brushed closely back from her forehead, and a headdress composed of a wreath of white jessamine and purple violets with long trailing vines completed a most recherché costume. The President, in his customary attire for such occasions, greeted the Cabinet, the for such occasions, greeted the Cabinet, the diplomatic corps, and the military, before occupying the place reserved for his party. His eldest son, Captain Robert Todd Lincoln, was in the ballroom for a considerable part of the evening with a beautiful daughter of Senator James Harlan. Since his graduation from Har-

vard in 1864, Robert had been serving on the staff of Lieutenant General Grant.

Shortly after midnight, the Presidential party was escorted to the supper room and seated at the head of a table before the doors were thrown open for other guests. "The onset of the crowd upon the tables was frightful," read one account, "and nothing but the immense reserves of eatables laid out by the thoughtful supper committee would have supplied the demand, or rather the waste. Numbers, who could not find immediate room at the tables, colonized in the numerous alcoves where they were catered for by some of their friends, with more audacity than good taste. The latter could be seen snatching whole *pâtés,* chickens, legs of veal, halves of turkeys, ornamental pyramids, etc., from the tables, and, bearing them aloft over the heads of the shuddering crowd (ladies especially, with greasy ruin to their dresses impending), carry them off in triumph for private delectation.

"The floor of the supper room was soon sticky, pasty, and oily with wasted confections, wasted cake, and debris of fowl and meat. The alcove appropriators of estates from the tables left their plates upon the floor after a free and easy sort, miscellaneously or in chance piles, adding to the difficulty of locomotion; and gentlemen, in conscientiously giving a wide berth to a lady's skirt, not infrequently steered clear of Scylla only to fall upon Charybdis of greasy crockery. Finally everybody was satisfied, even those who felt bound to 'eat their ten dollars worth,' and the ballroom again filled up, and the dance and promenade was resumed."

During this mêlée, a squabble occurred among employees in the kitchen which called for the interference of the police. Hearing the cooks swearing at one another, an officer entered just in time to see the most boisterous of the group struck by a large plate of chicken salad thrown by another of the "kitchen cabinet." The injured one, having been responsible for the rumpus, was taken before a Justice of the Peace who fined him one dollar and lectured him upon the impropriety of his conduct.

168

Campbell Hospital on Boundry Street (Florida Avenue) at the northern limit of Fifth and Sixth Streets, Northwest. Ambulances approach buildings beyond tents at upper left while army supply wagons pass the main entrance. *National Archives.*

President Lincoln and party left the Inaugural Ball about one o'clock but most of the guests lingered for hours afterwards, and others did not leave until daylight. The scene from the upper steps of the Patent Office, as groups departed, was unique. Powerful lights from reflectors threw long glares in every direction, and hacks "by the score" could be seen as far away as the eye could reach. One gentleman, who was anxiously inquiring for his carriage, was informed by some of the "jebus" (Negroes) that his vehicle was somewhere in the vicinity of the Treasury Department, and would probably be able to work its way up to the Patent Office in the course of the forenoon. Hackmen were making the most of the situation and charging large fees

for conveying parties to their destinations. The police arrested several who demanded as much as twenty-five dollars from those who had fallen into their clutches for short rides to nearby hotels.

The ordeal of attending the ball may have affected the President's health, for a few days later it was reported that he had sufficiently recovered from his severe indisposition to be in his office, but still was not well, and therefore received no one but members of the Cabinet and Senators on urgent business. Probably his continued ill-health prevented him from going to an afternoon performance for soldiers at Campbell Hospital of *Still Waters Run Deep,* starring the popular actors, E. L. Davenport and J. W. Wallack. More evidence, at a later date, of Wilkes Booth's plot to kidnap Lincoln went far in proving that the group of conspirators actually banded together on that occasion and followed a carriage supposed to be taking the President to the performance. Finding someone else in his place, they scattered, but several of them came together again at Mrs. Surratt's home to bemoan their failure and disappointment.

On March 17 one newspaper commented: "Although the President is yet quite feeble, he is slowly gaining strength, and yesterday afternoon he took a short ride, appearing upon the Avenue in his carriage, accompanied by his son Master Tad. If the thousands of office seekers who are now here besetting him upon every side would allow him to obtain a few days' relaxation, he would doubtless speedily recover his usual health; but notwithstanding the President's indisposition and the fact that this is Cabinet day, the White House was thronged again this morning with parties eager to obtain an interview."

That afternoon Lincoln appeared before a large gathering at the National Hotel and presented a rebel garrison flag, captured by an Indiana regiment at Fort Anderson, North Carolina, to Governor Morton of Indiana. The flag was unfurled over a balcony where Lincoln, the Governor, and several officers of the Indiana Volunteers (recently released from Confederate prisons) had assembled. After much cheering and a short speech by Governor Morton, the President said:

"It will be but a very few words that I shall undertake to say. I was born in Kentucky; raised in Indiana, and live in Illinois [laughter], and I now am here, where it is my business to be, to care equally for the good people of all the States. I am glad to see an Indiana regiment on this day able to present this captured flag to the Governor of the State of Indiana [applause]. I am not disposed, in saying this, to make distinction between the States, for all have done equally well [applause]. There are but few views or aspects of this great war upon which I have not said or written something whereby my own views might be made known. There is one: the recent attempt of our erring brethren, as they are sometimes called [laughter], to employ the Negro to fight for them. I have neither written nor made a speech upon that subject, because that was their business and not mine; and if I had a wish upon the subject, I had not the power to introduce it or make it effective.

"The great question with them was whether the Negro, being put into the army, will fight for them. I do not know, and therefore cannot decide [laughter]. They ought to know better than we, and do know. I have in my lifetime heard many arguments why the Negro ought to be a slave; but if they fight for those who would keep them in slavery, it will be a better argument than any I have yet heard [laughter and applause]. He who will fight for that ought to be a slave [applause]. They have concluded, at last, to take one out of four of the slaves and put him in the army; and that one out of four, who will fight to keep the others in slavery, ought to be a slave himself, unless he is killed in the fight [applause]. While I have often said that all men ought to be free, yet I would allow those colored persons to be slaves who want to be; and next to them those white men who argue in favor of making other people slaves [applause]. I am in favor of giving an opportunity to such white men to try it for themselves [applause]. I will say one thing in regard to the Negro being employed to fight for them that I do know. I know he cannot fight and stay at home and make bread too [laughter and applause], and as one is about as important as the other to them, I don't care which they do [renewed applause]. I am rather in favor of having them try as soldiers [applause]. They lack one vote of doing that, and I wish I could send my vote over the river, so that I might cast it in favor of allowing the Negro to fight [applause]. But they cannot fight and work both. We must now see the bottom of the enemy's resources. They will stand out as long as they can, and if the Negro will fight for them, they must allow him to fight. They have drawn upon their last branch of resources [applause], and we can now see the bottom [applause]. I am glad to see the end so near at hand [applause]. I

Negro infantry at Fort Lincoln, named for the President. Some 104,000 Negroes enlisted in the Union Army (1861-1865). *National Archives.*

The method of punishing Negro soldiers for various offenses was often the same as that given to white soldiers, with the exception that stacked rifles with long bayonets pointing upward warned the Negro not to fall from his perch. *Library of Congress.*

A photograph of Lincoln taken by H. F. Warren on the balcony of the White House, March 6, 1865, two days after his second inauguration. *Library of Congress.*

have said now more than I intended to, and will, therefore, bid you goodbye."

As Lincoln left the balcony, there were more cheers, and music by the band. To many present, he still appeared to be in ill-health, and after receiving the greetings of a few personal friends in the parlor of the hotel, he returned to the White House. It was upon this occasion that Wilkes Booth, then living at the hotel, mingled in the crowd swarming

about Lincoln's carriage, and watched him with such a demoniacal expression that his hatred of the President was noticed by those standing nearby. It was also while Lincoln was speaking that a girl named Lizzy Murty, who resided there and was known as "the genuine Secesh," tried to spit upon his head. Not until Lincoln was dead were the facts known and the girl taken into custody.

Directly across the street from the rear room

172

Howard's Livery Stable directly across the street from the room John Wilkes Booth occupied at the National Hotel. *Library of Congress.*

The National Hotel at Sixth Street and Pennsylvania Avenue where John Wilkes Booth was living when Lincoln spoke from a balcony (probably the one at right) and "Secesh" Lizzy Murty tried to spit upon his head. *Columbia Historical Society.*

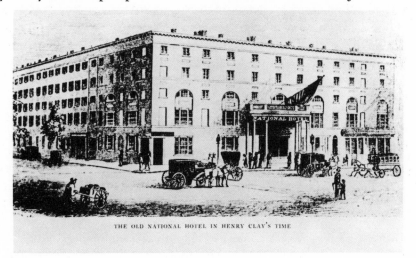

THE OLD NATIONAL HOTEL IN HENRY CLAY'S TIME

Booth occupied in the hotel was Howard's Livery Stable. When he wanted to hire a saddle horse, he opened his window, whistled to Howard, or an employee, who had a horse ready for him as requested. It is probable that Howard, on the day of the assassination, was unable to supply the right horse for him, and he therefore engaged the fast-running small bay mare, on which he escaped southward, from the Pumphrey stable.

About this time, Booth and the group plotting Lincoln's abduction met at Gotier's Restaurant on Pennsylvania Avenue between Twelfth and Thirteenth streets, Northwest. Gotier advertised that he was prepared to furnish dinner and supper parties for any number of gentlemen in a style equal to their desire for such entertainment, and that the best of provisions, obtained in larger cities, were forwarded to him by express. He boasted that his suites of parlors and dining-rooms, his wines and liquors, his table arrangements, cooks, servants, etc., were unsurpassed by any similar establishment in the United States. It was an elegant place for Booth to take his band of ruffians.

The session lasted far into the night. Arnold said the plan to abduct the President was impractical, and Surratt feared government officials had knowledge of the plot. Since no agreement seemed possible among them, it was suggested that the project be dropped. Booth, infuriated, banged his fist upon a table and exclaimed, "If the worst comes to the worst, I shall know what to do!" Before the meeting ended, however, all were congenial again and went their separate ways.

One of the better class of "fancy houses" catering to gentlemen seeking pleasure was kept by Nellie Turner Starr on Ohio Avenue, not far from the Smithsonian Institution. Although Booth was engaged to marry Bessie Hale, the pretty, buxom daughter of former Senator John P. Hale of New Hampshire, he often stayed with Nellie's sister Ella. She too was an attractive woman and knew how to soothe Booth when he got into one of his tantrums. Frustration of his plans to kidnap the President was making him more and more bitter in his denunciations against Lincoln and the Federal Government, and some of his friends were finding it difficult to get along with him. But in shooting galleries where he showed off his marksmanship, in cheap saloons where he was patronized by bartenders and ordinary habitués, and with Ella, he gratified his ego with pompous words and gestures.

Booth had promised John McCullough, a well-known actor, to appear with him at Ford's Theatre on his closing night. Bronchial trouble was still threatening Booth's stage appearances and the announcement that he would take the part of Pascara in *The Apostate* said, "If he shall be well, and in good voice, we venture to predict that he will create a sensation." It was his last performance.

A newspaper account of Union victories told of an Arabian horse, belonging to Jefferson Davis, which had just been captured by Sherman's scouts. The animal, a gift to Davis

from the Viceroy of Egypt, had been brought over on a Confederate blockade runner and taken into the interior of North Carolina for safe keeping. The scouts announced their intention of sending it to President Lincoln, but it never reached him. Following this news were the prophetic words:

"THE PRESIDENT'S HEALTH—We believe it was quite possible to have selected a stronger man for President; yet that does not conflict with the fact that his death or permanent disability now would be a calamity very generally and justly deplored. We cannot forecast the future which that bereavement would open; yet we think few Americans, even though disloyal, can wish to confront its realization.

"But, if the President is to outlive the term on which he has just entered, a radical retrenchment must be promptly effected in the current exactions on his time and energies. He has been carried further toward the grave by his four years in the White House than he could have been by ten years of constant labor in the courts or on a farm. All who knew him in 1860 and have met him in 1865 must have observed his air of fatigue, exhaustion and languor—so different from his old hearty, careless, jovial manner....

"For human strength is finite, and no man could endure the constant tension of his faculties imposed on President Lincoln without a more or less speedy breakdown. Go when you will to the White House, from early morn until late at night, and you will find the antechamber filled with a crowd of eager solicitors of a special interview with the President.... Let it be understood that if the President would confer for even two minutes with everyone who might fancy that he had an occasion for an interview, Mr. Lincoln could not remain above ground for even a month longer." Within that month he was to be shot down by an assassin's bullet.

Despite his apparent ill-health, the President left Washington on the steamer *River Queen* for the front. In company with General Grant, he rode from City Point to witness the fighting in that area. Rumors spread that this trip had to do with a desire for peace by Confederate authorities, and that Lincoln had

Waiting outside the Cabinet room in the White House to see Mr. Lincoln. *National Park Service*.

GLORY!!!

HAIL COLUMBIA!!!

HALLELUJAH!!!

RICHMOND OURS!!!

LEE'S RETREAT CUT OFF!

OFFICIAL WAR BULLETIN.

WAR DEPARTMENT,
WASHINGTON, April 3, 10.45 a. m.

Major General Dix, New York:

LATER.

It appears from a dispatch of Gen. Weitzel, just received by this Department, that our forces under his command are in Richmond, having taken it at 8.█ this morning.

EDWIN M. STANTON, Secretary of War.

GRANT.

The exhilerating news from the front sent by President Lincoln to Secretary Stanton yesterday, and which was duly issued by us in an extra *Star*, was the subject of general gratification throughout the city, and our office was thronged with people anxious for authentic particulars, such as conveyed in the War Department bulletins.

By the despatches received since, by Secretary Stanton, it will be seen that the news grows better and better hour by hour.

OUR CAPTURES.

Orders were received here to-day by the proper athorities to prepare for the reception of a large number of captured officers, who will be forwarded to this city immediately from City Point. The enlisted men will be

Washington Evening Star

met with their representatives in Hampton Roads. The newspapers carried no startling headlines, but a day later one asked:

"Has Richmond been evacuated? This is the question on the street today, started, it would seem, by the fact that no Richmond papers of Wednesday were received here this morning, and hence the conclusions jumped at, that newspapers, Lee's army, Jefferson Davis and the whole rebel paraphernalia have decamped for less straitened quarters. The report needs confirmation, decidedly, but will do to gamble on."

The gamble was good. Early on the morning of April 3, Secretary of War Stanton had received a telegram from City Point. It read: "This morning General Grant reports Petersburg evacuated and he is confident Richmond also is. He is pushing forward to cut off, if possible, the retreating army. A. Lincoln."

Newspapers, with columns headed EXTRA were read and tossed into the air by excited

This Civil War photograph showing boxes of "Army Bread" doled out to soldiers was captioned "Hard Tack." *National Archives.*

citizens. "PETERSBURG COMPLETELY INVESTED! Our Troops Sweeping Everything Before Them! Fifty Cannon And 12,000 Prisoners Captured! Petersburg Ours!" Two hours later Stanton issued a statement at the War Department: "It appears, from a dispatch of Gen. Weitzel just received by this Department, that our forces under his command are in Richmond having taken it at 8:15 this morning."

Throughout the city people were shouting, "Glory Hallelujah! Hail Columbia! Richmond Ours!" and soldiers were yelling "No more hardtack!" One newsman graphically described events of that day. "As we write Washington City is in such a blaze of excitement and enthusiasm as we never before witnessed here in any approachable degree. The thunder of cannon; the ringing of bells; the eruption of flags from every window and housetop; the shouts of enthusiastic gatherings on the streets, all echo the glorious re-

port, Richmond is ours!!!" The report that Lincoln had gone to Richmond was wildly cheered everywhere.

The news started the city off on a series of celebrations which were to end in tragedy and mourning. Secretary of State Seward recommended that all public buildings be illuminated in honor of the capture of Richmond. Home owners were called upon to do the same, and the idea grew to a plan for a "Grand Illumination" at a later date. Union flags were brought out, speeches were made, bands paraded, and crowds surged through the streets singing and shouting, with little interference from civic or military authorities. Police tolerantly permitted them to have their own way, and arrested only pranksters who committed flagrant outrages. Those too intoxicated to take care of themselves were taken home, some requiring this service several times during the night.

At the Marine Barracks, news of the capture

The Marine Band and troops on the parade ground of their barracks in Washington during the Civil War. Commandant's quarters are at right. *U. S. Defense Department (Marine Corps).*

The band of the 10th Veteran Reserve Corps, and many others, joined in Washington parades celebrating the end of the war. *Library of Congress.*

Group from the Marine Corps line up for a photograph. *Library of Congress.*

created great excitement among the officers and soldiers quartered there. The resplendent uniforms they wore, and a certain air of superiority, always attracted females. During the afternoon and evening many of them visited the Marines in their reception rooms where the singing and dancing continued far into the night. Emory Hospital convalescents heard the news just as they were leaving mess, and all who were able, including many cripples, went out to the green and cheered for Grant and the Union forces. Patients at other hospitals, well enough to "stand a holiday" were given passes. Schools throughout the city held patriotic programs and then were dismissed until the next morning.

On the night of the first illumination, the city was flooded with light. The glare of fireworks, inspiring music (bands were playing in every downtown street), and the declamations of popular speakers, kept the celebration at a high pitch. The War Department was a brilliant spectacle with powerful colored lights in the court streaming upward to illuminate flags, mottoes, and other decorations. A prominent feature in a window above the main entrance of the Navy Department was a large size model of a full-rigged man-of-war. Over the entrance of the State Department were the words: PEACE AND GOODWILL TO ALL NATIONS BUT NO ENTANGLING ALLIANCES AND NO FOREIGN INTERVENTION, and above the northern entrance, AT HOME UNION IS ORDER, AND ORDER IS PEACE. ABROAD UNION IS STRENGTH, AND STRENGTH IS PEACE.

The one hundred and ten windows of the Treasury Department fronting the Avenue sparkled with twelve lights each, and at its eastern entrance spread a replica of a ten-dollar compound-interest Treasury note bearing the caption, U. S. GREENBACKS—GRANT GIVES THE GREENBACKS A METALLIC RING. The White House, aglow with light, made a fitting central figure in the grand display of these public buildings. The gleaming Capitol, with the United States flag crowning a lighted dome, and the large motto, THIS IS THE LORD'S DOING, IT IS MARVELOUS IN OUR EYES, drew the attention of all spectators. The City Hall, business buildings, and private residences, all flamed with lights and patriotic decorations.

It had been announced that Vice President Johnson would speak in front of the Patent Office building that night. By eight o'clock the

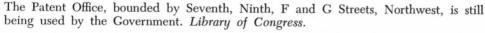

The Patent Office, bounded by Seventh, Ninth, F and G Streets, Northwest, is still being used by the Government. *Library of Congress.*

entire space was filled with people packed together as closely as they could stand, while hundreds of men and boys perched on the steps or clung to the cornices and railings. Gas pipes shaped in large letters to form the word UNION flared at one side of the building while fireworks flashed above brilliantly lighted windows throughout the area. Gaily decorated carriages arrived and departed, weaving a fantastic fringe of many colors around the vast assemblage. To the right of the main entrance, a platform had been built over the granite slabs for the Vice President and his guests. Their arrival was greeted with loud cheers and patriotic music.

After several distinguished residents had spoken briefly, the Vice President was introduced. He dwelt upon the necessity of the proper punishment of rebel leaders who had forced the youth of the South into a strife they had feared to share. Treason should be put in its proper light, he said, as the greatest of crimes. While magnanimity and mercy were to be given to the deluded masses, he believed signal and memorable punishment should be dealt to the crafty instigators and bloody leaders, their property confiscated and used to remunerate the loyal men whom they had despoiled and persecuted. He declared the war had clearly established the fact that in the people of a free country dwells greater strength than in more centralized absolution. Other speakers followed the Vice President and the meeting broke up with more cheers and music.

Crowds had been orderly and no serious accidents or offenses marred the celebration. Due to the extraordinary number of drunkards on the streets, however, Superintendent of Police A. C. Richards had all sergeants retain the day-men on their beats until eleven P.M. to serve with the night force. This led one newspaper to remark "Some jokers started the report that Superintendent Richards had given orders that any person found sober on the streets after nine o'clock on so joyful an occasion, would be arrested, and perhaps it was to duly qualify themselves against such arrest that so many got hilarious." But several did end up in jail. At a restaurant on Ninth Street, Northwest, while patrons of the cup were expressing their joy over the success of the Union army, two men began eulogizing Jefferson Davis and cursing Abe Lincoln and the Federal Government in general. "It was well for them," the press commented, "that they were arrested, for in the excitement of the hour there was a strong probability that both would have been roughly handled by loyal men."

That evening Lincoln was still at City Point. At noon the next day Mrs. Lincoln, accompanied by Senator Charles Sumner and Senator James Harlan and family, left on the steamer *Monohansett* to join him. There they heard of the painful accident to Secretary Seward during a runaway in Washington. Starting out for a drive, the Secretary and his two grown children, Fanny and Frederick, stopped at the home of a Miss Titus who was to join the party. As she entered the carriage, the driver, holding the reins in his hands, got down from his box to shut the door. The horses became restless and Frederick went to quiet them. Suddenly they reared and galloped off, knocking him to the ground and jerking the lines from the driver. As they bolted into a side street, the Secretary jumped from the carriage and suffered fractures of the right arm and jaw. The horses then ran into a yard where one of them fell and brought the runaway to a halt, allowing the two women to alight in safety.

The Secretary's accident was a shock to Washington residents since first reports intimated that it might prove fatal. The general feeling that Seward's loss would be irreparable to the country was mingled with their high personal regard for him. Had Seward remained in the carriage with the young women, he would have escaped injury; had he escaped injury, he probably would have been murdered the following week.

Newspapers continued to feature accounts of the occupation of Richmond, the whereabouts of Grant and Lee, and speculations on the eventual surrender of the South. Washington was being overrun with Confederate deserters, and a rebel band that had come into the Union lines at Petersburg arrived in the city, took the oath of allegiance, and became known as "Hackerston's Rebel Brigade Band" in honor of their leader. They attracted a great deal of attention as they marched from the wharf at the head of one hundred and seventy additional deserters, playing "Old Virginia Shore," "Dan Tucker," "Jordan," and other Southern tunes. When asked to play the national airs, they expressed regrets, saying they had not been permitted to play them during the war and would have to practice before being able to do so again.

In front of General Augur's office they played a medley of old-fashioned Negro tunes and were loudly applauded. From there, they proceeded to the War Department to pay their compliments to Secretary Stanton. Taking a position in the north yard of the building, just as the employees were leaving, they played "Ain't We Glad To Get Out Of The Wilderness" and "Dixie." So many people gathered to hear them, some on horseback or in vehicles, that street traffic was almost at a standstill. When the music ended, General E. D. Townsend, on behalf of the Secretary, extended his thanks for their efforts and welcomed them "beneath the folds of the Star Spangled Banner." At the Metropolitan Hotel they serenaded the wife of General Winfield Scott Hancock and were invited in for refreshments. Later they were furnished with transportation and left for their homes in other cities.

About nine o'clock on the evening of April 9, the President, Mrs. Lincoln and Tad, with other members of their party, returned to Washington on the steamer *River Queen*. The President's brief relief from annoying political duties in the capital seemed to have had a beneficial effect for his health and spirits were excellent. As the Lincolns rode from the wharf they saw bonfires burning in the streets and excited crowds at many points along the way. Tad, being curious, called out and asked what was happening. A man, taking no note of those in the carriage, answered, "Why, where have you been? Lee has surrendered." Lee and Grant had met at Appomattox that day.

Early next morning, Lee's surrender was fully and officially announced by the roar of

D. C., MONDAY, APRIL 10, 1865;

SURRENDER OF LEE AND HIS WHOLE ARMY!

Grant's Terms Accepted!

ALL THE ARMS, ARTILLERY, AND PUBLIC PROPERTY TURNED OVER TO OUR GOVERNMENT.

OFFICERS AND MEN PAROLED.

THE OFFICERS ALLOWED THEIR SIDE ARMS AND HORSES.

LEE'S ARMY PERMITTED TO RETURN HOME.

THE CORRESPONDENCE.

GRANT WISHES TO SPARE LIFE.

LEE DESIRES THE RESTORATION OF PEACE.

CONGRATULATORY ORDER OF SECRETARY STANTON.

A GRAND SALUTE TO BE FIRED IN EVERY PART OF THE UNION.

OFFICIAL WAR BULLETIN.

WAR DEPARTMENT,
WASHINGTON, D. C., April 9, 1865, 9 p. m.
Major General John A. Dix, New York:

This Department has just received official report of the surrender, this day, of General Lee and his army to Lieutenant General Grant, on the terms proposed by General Grant. Details will be given as speedily as possible.

EDWIN M. STANTON, Secretary of War.

HEADQ'RS ARMIES OF UNITED STATES,
April 9, 9.40 p. m.

Hon. Edwin M. Stanton, Secretary of War:

General Lee surrendered the army of Northern Virginia this afternoon upon terms pro-

Washington Evening Star

181

artillery and the ringing of bells. Under the bold-faced heading EXTRA, Washington read: "When Lee, the wisest and bravest of the Confederate leaders, sees no ray of hope for the Confederate cause, and voluntarily lays down his arms to prevent the further and futile effusion of blood, the most incredulous optimist amongst his followers must accept his judgment as decisive. We may now expect to hear at any moment of the surrender of Johnson and his army, and most of the scattered remnants of the Confederate military organization throughout the South will follow as soon as the news of the capitulation of their military chief is known."

All government departments closed for the day, and wild jubilant throngs poured through the streets. Soldiers on duty at the Central Signal Station on top of the Winter Building at Seventeenth Street and Pennsylvania Avenue, Northwest, and elsewhere, were permitted to leave their posts and join in the celebration. Navy Yard men, accompanied by a band, paraded down the Avenue with two well-preserved howitzers in tow, which were fired at intervals. Treasury clerks, who had marched to the White House singing patriotic songs, were there when the Navy Yard men rushed into the grounds and, amid the cheering thousands, boomed a salute for the President. In a few moments Lincoln appeared and said:

"I am very much rejoiced, my friends, in the fact that an occasion has occurred so pleasurable that the people find it impossible to refrain from giving vent to their feelings [applause]. I suppose that arrangements are being made for a formal demonstration either this or tomorrow evening [a voice—That's too late!]. Should such demonstration take place I, of course, will be expected to respond, if called upon, and if I permit you to dribble all out of me now, I will have nothing left to say on that occasion [laughter and applause].

"I observe that you have a band of music with you. I propose having this interview closed by the band performing a particular tune, which I will name. Before this is done, however, I wish to mention one or two little circumstances connected with it. I have al-

ways thought that 'Dixie' was one of the best tunes I had ever heard. Our adversaries over the way, I know, have attempted to appropriate it, but I insist that on yesterday we fairly captured it [applause]. I referred the question to the Attorney General and he gave it as his legal opinion that it is now our property [laughter and loud applause]. I now ask the band to favor us with its performance." So the band struck up "Dixie," the crowd cheered, the howitzers boomed again, and the President retired.

Mayor Wallach had requested the loan of a battery from the War Department, and at noon it appeared in front of the City Hall to fire a salute of two hundred rounds in the presence of an immense gathering which included many city officials. During the afternoon and evening the mayor, civic leaders, members of the Cabinet, and high-ranking military officers threw open their doors to friends, and the multitude continued to surge in and out of the White House grounds. Again Lincoln was called upon for a speech and appeared at a window to say that he could only repeat what he had said earlier in the day, that, in consequence of the glorious news a general demonstration was being planned, he hoped for the following evening, when he would be "much better prepared to say what I have to say than I am now or can be this evening." Then he added, "Everything I say, you know, goes into print [laughter and applause]. If I make a mistake it doesn't merely affect me nor you but the country. I, therefore, ought at least to try not to make mistakes [voices: You have made no mistakes yet!]. If, then, a general demonstration be made tomorrow evening, and it be agreeable, I will endeavor to say something, and not make a mistake, without at least trying to avoid it [laughter and applause]. Thanking you for the compliment of this call, I bid you good evening."

The speech alluded to by the President was given the following evening before thousands who not only filled the grounds facing the brilliantly illuminated White House, but completely obstructed the sidewalks and the Avenue bordering it. They were enthusiastic and in good humor, standing patiently in the deep mud and misty drizzle until the President was seen at a window over the main entrance. Then they cheered with all their might and repeated their noisy greeting when Mrs. Lincoln appeared at another window with some friends.

For this occasion the President had prepared with deliberation, and read from a manuscript copy a speech which would give no chance for misconception of his views. It related to the establishment of national authority and the best policy to be pursued by the Government toward the states and people in rebellion. He referred to the "Louisiana Plan" as the one most likely to result in a thorough and reliable pacification in the shortest time. The plan admitted all the people of the South not obnoxious to the charge of having been prime originators of the rebellion, or leading workers in it, to resume their former relations to the states and general Government, just as soon as they came forward to avail themselves of the opportunity. It pre-

vented all others from practicing any profession, business, or trade within the limits of the state, and thus compelled them to migrate where they could not possibly work future injury to the public welfare. It also adopted the local laws to the altered conditions of the Negro population to improve and speedily benefit the community at large. That he favored permitting them to vote startled two men in the audience. "That means nigger citizenship," exclaimed Wilkes Booth to David Herold. "Now, by God, I'll put him through!"

The President introduced Senator James Harlan who made a brief speech and asked what was to be done with "these [Southern] brethren of ours?" Instantly, a chorus of voices shouted, "Hang 'em! Hang 'em!" His reference to the President's power to pardon them drew cries of "Never! Never!" But his willingness "to trust the future in the hands of the first citizen of the Republic, who has been elevated a second time, to see that the laws are faithfully executed," brought loud and prolonged cheering. After music by sev-

Now Lincoln could write:

Mathew Brady, sitting on ground at left, carefully carried his photographic equipment, including glass plates, in this outfit as he followed the Army from battlefield to battlefield. *National Archives.*

eral bands, the crowd separated, many going to the home of Secretary Stanton which was brilliantly lighted and magnificently decorated with large flags, flowers, and evergreens. Patriotic tunes greeted the Secretary as he returned from the War Department to receive a noisy ovation. On the upper steps to his house, he paused and called for cheers for "The President of the *whole* United States." Following huzzas for General Grant and the armies of the Potomac and the James, the Secretary received a final round of applause and entered his home.

At this time, Matthew Brady, the enterprising photographer, had on view at his Washington studio a large assortment of pictures, made while following the Union army, and others taken from negatives found in Richmond. Among them were copies of prominent Confederate Generals, including Lee and Stonewall Jackson, and a large panoramic scene made by him of the entire city, showing the burned part, Belle Isle, the prisons, and pontoon bridges across the James River.

Although most government buildings and private residences continued to be brightly lighted at night, a "General Illumination invited by the City Councils" was announced for April 13. That it far exceeded any previous demonstration was evident when all the city's lights tore away the darkness. Descriptions of the event verged on the poetic: "The very heavens seemed to have come down, and the stars twinkled in a sort of faded way, as if the solar systems were out of order, and the earth had become the great luminary. Everybody illuminated."

Throughout the night, revelers paraded up and down the Avenue and streets with music adding to the gaiety. News that Mobile, Alabama, had been taken over by Union troops was greeted with loud cheers. The scene as viewed from the City Hall was one of the most impressive ever witnessed in Washington during the years Lincoln lived there. In every direction "long rows of illuminated windows blended into one, and presented an unbroken wall of flame." Georgetown, Alexandria, and the surrounding heights added to the vastness of the spectacle by their gorgeous displays. One reporter boasted: "It would have been creditable indeed to the great commercial cities in which the wealth of a single block exceeds all in Washington. No more need be said in behalf of the citizens' demonstration than the admitted fact that grand as was the display by the Government (which so promptly and kindly co-operated with the city authorities), it was only auxiliary to that of the city, so general in its character and so brilliant was the latter."

Yet, in the midst of all this hilarity and light, there lurked the shadow of an impending tragedy. And one man at least, because of illness, could not join the merrymakers. Steel bandages had been placed around the lower part of Secretary Seward's face and neck to support the jawbone fractured when he jumped from the carriage during the runaway. The swelling had reduced, he did not suffer so much pain but still was unable to leave his room. As talking was very difficult for him, he had to use a slate and pencil to communicate with others. Fate stood at his bedside.

Specters' Rendezvous

Good Friday was not a pleasant day in Washington. Dark clouds hovered above the festively decorated city and in late afternoon the air grew damp and chilly. Reports that the Stars and Stripes again flew over Fort Sumter, as Union troops marched in, renewed the excitement. Downtown streets were crowded, and drunken rowdies continued to take advantage of the holiday laxity. That morning Captain Robert Lincoln and several of General Grant's staff arrived by steamer bringing their military effects and

Headquarters of Lieutenant-General Grant, across from the War Department, on Seventeenth Street, Northwest. It has recently been torn down and the site is now a parking lot. *National Park Service.*

horses. Grant, who preceded them the day before, was to establish his permanent headquarters in the capital.

About noon an item appeared in the Washington *Star* which was the cue for John Wilkes Booth's mad act. It read: "FORD'S THEATER— 'Honor To Our Soldiers,' a new and patriotic song and chorus has been written by Mr. H. B. Phillips, and will be sung this evening by the entire company to do honor to Lieutenant General Grant and President Lincoln and lady, who visit the theatre in compliment to

General Grant reports to Secretary Stanton at the War Department. *Washington Public Library.*

Two items in the *Washington Evening Star* of April 14, 1865, relate to the President and General Grant.

Miss Laura Keene, whose benefit and last appearance is announced in the bills of the day. The music of the above song is composed by Prof. W. Withers, Jr." Other notices that Lincoln and Grant would attend the performance appeared elsewhere.

The information sank deeply into Booth's brain, twisting it into a bold decision. Plans and efforts to abduct the President had been futile. Lee had surrendered. Now the tyrant Lincoln would send his bloodhounds into the South to destroy the last vestige of a proud but defeated people. Time was running out. Something had to be done—quickly. On that afternoon of April 14, the idea which had haunted Booth on several occasions returned to hold him fast. Once again he would act— in a theatre—on the stage! For this he need not strain his voice; there would be only a few words to speak, but the performance must be flawless.

Hurriedly, Booth gathered together at the Herndon House the men he had chosen for the cast, and assigned each one the part he was to play. Paine was to kill Seward, Atzerodt was to murder Vice President Johnson, while he (Booth) would assassinate Lincoln. At the appointed time and place, Herold was to meet them and guide their escape southward. Apparently John Surratt was not in Washington that evening, but his role never has been definitely ascertained. It was later rumored he was to have assassinated General Grant.

During the afternoon the President and Mrs. Lincoln were seen taking a drive. At dusk the Arsenal employees' torchlight procession passed along the Avenue to the White

House, thence to the residence of Secretary Stanton and on to those of several other military leaders. Amusement places were beginning to fill up and at curtain time in Ford's Theatre, where Laura Keene was starring in *Our American Cousin,* an expectant audience awaited the arrival of the presidential party with General and Mrs. Grant.

At the White House, Lincoln had taken time to see some callers, and had scribbled on a card, which was to bear his last handwriting:

Allow Mr. Ashmun & friend to come in at 9- A.M. tomorrow—
A. Lincoln
April 14. 1865.

Thus delayed, the show went on without them. Not until the second act was the performance interrupted by the orchestra playing "Hail To The Chief" as Lincoln and his guests appeared in the box directly above the stage. Immediately all eyes turned in that direction expecting to see the General and Mrs. Grant, but instead, they saw only a young couple whom few recognized as Major Henry R. Rathbone and his fiancée, Miss Clara Harris, daughter of a New York senator. Late in the afternoon, the Grants had sent their regrets to the White House saying they would be billing over with affections, which I'm ready to pour out all over you like apple sass, over roast pork.

Mrs M Mr. Trenchard, you will please recollect you are addressing my daughter, and in my presence.

Asa Yes, I'm offering her my heart and hand just as she wants them, with nothing in 'em.

Mrs M Augusta, dear, to your room.   [*Exit, R.*

Aug Yes, ma, the nasty beast.

Mrs M I am aware, Mr. Trenchard, you are not used to the manners of good society, and that, alone, will excuse the impertinence of which you have been guilty.

Asa Don't know the manners of good society, eh? Well, I guess I know enough to turn you inside out, old gal—you sockdologizing old man-trap. Wal, now, when I think what I've thrown away in hard cash to-day I'm apt to call myself some awful hard names, 400,000 dollars is a big pile for a man to light his cigar with. If that gal had only given me herself in exchange, it would'nt have been a bad bargain, But I dare no more ask that gal to be my wife, than I dare ask Queen Victoria to dance a Cape Cod reel.

Enter FLORENCE, L. 1 E.

Flo What do you mean by doing all these dreadful things?

Asa Which things.

Flo Come here, sir.   [*He does so.*

Asa What's the matter?

Flo Do you know this piece of paper?   [*Showing burnt paper.*

Asa Well, I think I have seen it before. [*Aside*] Its old Mark Trenchard's will that I left half burned up like a landhead, that I am.

Flo And you're determined to give up this fortune to Mary Meredith.

Asa Well, I couldn't help it if I tried.

Flo Oh, don't say that.

Page from OUR AMERICAN COUSIN

unable to attend the performance for they were leaving the city to visit their children who were attending school in Burlington, New Jersey. The disappointment of the audience was shown by the mild applause which greeted the President and his unexpected guests.

The play continued until the second scene of the third act. Actor Henry Hawk, in the part of Asa Trenchard, had just said: "Don't know the manners of good society, eh? Well, I guess I know enough to turn you inside out, old gal, you sockdologizing old man-trap."

189

The audience roared with laughter. Suddenly the sharp report of a pistol was heard. For a moment many in the theatre believed some novelty had been interjected into the performance. A man shouted *"Sic semper tyrannis"* which few persons understood, leaped from the President's box, fell as he alighted on the stage, then hobbled across it brandishing a knife in his hand, and disappeared beyond the wings. He was of middle stature, dark hair and eyes, and wore a black mustache. Several persons in the audience thought the man was John Wilkes Booth. Members of the cast, who had darted from his path as he escaped, were sure it was Booth. Above the

"...Suddenly the sharp report of a pistol was heard." *National Park Service.*

"...A man hobbled across the stage, brandishing a knife in his hand." *National Park Service.*

Map of downtown Washington showing Booth's flight from Ford's Theatre to the old Navy Yard Bridge (Anacostia Bridge) and into southern Maryland. *National Park Service.*

confused audience, a woman's cry was heard: "The President has been shot. Is there a surgeon here?" It was the voice of Mrs. Lincoln in the upper box.

Turmoil followed. Part of the audience rushed toward the stage screaming, "Hang him! Hang him!" They believed it possible to capture the assassin, but by that time he had mounted the horse left in the rear of the theatre and was galloping in the direction of Maryland. Others surged toward the President's box but were stopped by shouts of "Stand back! Give him air! Has anyone stimulants?" Excitement grew, and there was diffi-

Lincoln is carried from Ford's Theatre to the home of William Petersen directly across the street. *National Park Service.*

Soldiers guarding the Petersen house, where Lincoln lay dying, and keeping back the crowds near the entrance. *Library of Congress.*

Payne attempts to assassinate Seward but is blocked on his way to the bedroom by the Secretary's son, Frederick. *National Park Service.*

culty in clearing a way so that the helpless form of the President could be carried directly across the street to the home of Mr. William Peterson. Someone yelled, "Burn the damned theatre!" but soldiers arrived and kept the mad throng in order. The hoofs of their horses clicked on the sidewalks, and their swords rattled. A strong guard also was stationed in front of the White House where a curious mob had gathered supposing the President would be brought back there.

In the midst of the clamor came news of the attempt to murder Secretary Seward. An assassin had entered his home, struck down members of his family and attendants, then tried to cut the Secretary's throat, but the steel bandage supporting his jaw had warded off the blow and saved his life. Secretaries Ed-

win Stanton, Gideon Wells, and other government officials, hearing the gruesome report, called at Seward's home and learned that the condition of each victim was critical. While there, they heard of the President's assassination and rushed off to the house where Lincoln lay dying, but had to push through the mad throng in the street before they could enter. For hours, carriages arrived and departed with men well known in public life who made their way to Peterson's door to inquire about the condition of the President.

At 2:30 A.M., April 15, 1865, it was announced that Lincoln was growing weaker. "The ball is lodged in his brain, three inches from where it entered the skull," read the bulletin. "He remains insensible, and his condition utterly hopeless. The Vice-President

Kirkwood House, Twelfth Street and Pennsylvania Avenue, Northwest, where Johnson lived. Atzerodt was to have assassinated him there. *National Park Service*

has been to see him, but all company except the Cabinet, his family and a few friends are rigidly excluded. Large crowds still continue in the street, as near to the house as the line of guards allow." But at the Kirkwood House, where Vice President Johnson lived, no one had been molested. The cowardly Atzerodt wanted nothing to do with murder, and had left Washington.

Rumors spread. Was the man who had shot down the President John Wilkes Booth? Yes and no. Who had wielded the knife at Seward's throat? Were conspirators at large in the city? Was there a plot to murder the entire Cabinet and all high-ranking military leaders? Everywhere there was confusion. The entire city presented a scene of wild excitement, accompanied by violent expressions of in-

Death-bed scene of Lincoln, as sketched immediately after his removal, by Herman Faber, a hospital steward, sent there as an artist to illustrate the medical war record. Details of those present and their positions, were given to Mr. Faber by several attending physicians who later approved of the drawing as to its correctness and accuracy. (Information from a letter by his son, Edwin F. Faber, to the University of Pennsylvania School of Medicine.) *Library of Congress*.

dignation and profound sorrow. Authorities seemed too stunned to get into action. Before they regained their wits, an early dawn was spreading over the housetops.

Orders were issued thick and fast. All travel was suspended. No one was permitted to leave Washington by foot, horseback, vehicle, rail or river transport. Pickets were stationed at intervals in the streets. Cavalry guarded roads leading into the surrounding country. Mounted men and military detectives scoured nearby rural areas. Homes and public buildings were searched. Scores of Confederate deserters who had taken the oath, and who roamed the streets at all times, suddenly disappeared and by Saturday not a gray uniform was to be seen except under guard. The secessionists residing in Washington and Georgetown were in some instances induced by their fear of public reprisal to drape their homes and maintain silence except in the presence of those whom they could trust as rebel sympathizers. Arrests were made. Many persons in the audience at Ford's Theatre on the night of the crime, members of the cast, stage hands, and other employees, were questioned.

Meanwhile the hands of a surgeon's watch were moving as he stood at Lincoln's bedside in the Peterson house that morning: 6:00—pulse failing, respiration 28; 6:30—still failing and labored breathing; 7:00—symptoms of immediate dissolution; 7:22—death!

Shortly after nine o'clock the remains of the nation's first martyred President were placed in a temporary coffin and carried by six young men of the Quartermaster's Department to the White House. An escort of cavalry accompanied them, followed by General C. C. Auger, commanding the Department of Washington, and several other military officers. The solemn procession moved slowly up Tenth Street to G, Northwest, and thence to the White House, while people along the route stood mute and uncovered. The gay decorations on public buildings and private dwellings had been removed and replaced by drapes of mourning. Even the most humble home was marked by some token of grief. Throughout the city, flags were at half-mast and bells tolled.

FROM OUR SPECIAL WAR CORRESPONDENT.

"CITY POINT, VA., *April* —, 8.30 A.M.
"All seems well with us."—A. LINCOLN.

This cartoon appeared in Harper's *Weekly* on April 15, 1865, the day Lincoln died. It refers to the surrender of Lee at Appomattox. *National Park Service.*

Washington Evening Star

EXTRA.

THE DEATH OF THE PRESIDENT.

At 22 minutes past seven o'clock the President breathed his last, closing his eyes as if falling to sleep, and his countenance assuming an expression of perfect serenity. There were no indications of pain, and it was not known that he was dead until the gradually decreasing respiration ceased altogether. Rev. Dr. Gurley, (of the New York Avenue Presbyterian Church,) immediately on its being ascertained that life was extinct, knelt at bedside and offered an

which was

General Grant received the news of Lincoln's assassination while at the Walnut Street Wharf in Philadelphia on the way to Burlington. Boarding a special train, he got into Washington at noon and immediately went to the White House. Shortly before his arrival, Andrew Johnson had taken the oath of office as the seventeenth President of the United States.

No more criticisms now of Lincoln's state papers, speeches, actions, his jokes and awkward mannerisms, his tall, gaunt figure and homely smile. No more criticisms—only the words of the poet Walt Whitman to read and remember:

O Captain! my Captain! our fearful trip is done;
The ship has weather'd every rack, the prize we
  sought is won;
The Port is near, the bells I hear, the people all
  exulting,
While follow eyes the steady keel, the vessel grim
  and daring:
  But O heart! heart! heart!
    O the bleeding drops of red,
      Where on the deck my Captain lies,
        Fallen cold and dead.

O Captain! my Captain! rise up and hear the bells;
Rise up—for you the flag is flung—for you the bugle
  trills;
For you bouquets and ribbon'd wreaths—for you
  the shores a-crowding;
For you they call, the swaying mass, their eager
  faces turning;
  Here Captain! dear father!
    This arm beneath your head;
      It is some dream that on the deck,
        You've fallen cold and dead.

My Captain does not answer, his lips are pale and
  still;
My father does not feel my arm, he has no pulse
  nor will;
The ship is anchor'd safe and sound, its voyage
  closed and done;
  Exult, O shores, and ring, O bells!
    But I, with mournful tread,
      Walk the deck my Captain lies,
        Fallen cold and dead.

Newspapers, in their accounts of the criminal events, attempted to separate facts from fables, but a few excerpts indicate how wrong were many of the reports they doled out to

the public. One said in part: "Every exertion has been made to prevent the escape of the murderer. His horse has been found on the road near Washington. . . . It appears from a letter found in Booth's trunk [at the National Hotel where Booth had lived] that the murder was planned before the fourth of March, but fell through because the accomplice backed out until Richmond could be heard from. . . . One of them [the assassins] has evidently made his way to Baltimore, the other has not yet been traced. . . ."

Another stated that John Surratt, "who it is believed did the bloody work at Secretary Seward's, has for many years been branded as a desperado of the worst character. A suit was brought against him by a young lady residing across the Eastern Branch, for seduction, and so desperate was his character that for some time the officers were afraid to serve the writ; but one of them by laying in ambush succeeded in taking him. . . ." A third added: "As it is suspected that this conspiracy originated in Maryland, the telegraph flashed the mournful news to Balitmore, and all the cavalry was immediately put upon active duty. Every road was picketed and every precaution taken to prevent the escape of the assassins."

The fourth bordered on the ludicrous. Word that the criminals were still in the city, disguised as women, resulted in four men, dressed in female attire, being arrested in Georgetown and committed to the Old Capitol Prison. The men were only pleasure bent.

A number of rebel sympathizers, noting the inability of officials to track down Lincoln's assassin, became brazen. A few did not hesitate to approve the deed, and tauntingly proposed to "illuminate." In so short a time, there were sections of the city where the murder of the President was a mockery. Confederate gray uniforms, worn by deserters who had taken the oath to the Union, also were seen again upon the streets.

Some truth, however, began filtering through to the people of Washington. Colonel Lafayette C. Baker, Special Detective of the War Department, who organized and was the first chief of the United States Secret Service, sat in his office opposite Willard's

Andrew Johnson taking the oath of office as seventeenth President of the United States, in the small parlor of the Kirkwood house. *Library of Congress.*

Colonel Lafayette C. Baker, in his office opposite Willard's Hotel, outlines his plans to capture John Wilkes Booth, and other so-called conspirators. At his right is his cousin, Lieutenant Luther B. Baker. *Library of Congress.*

Headquarters of Provost Marshal General Christopher C. Augur on the corner of Seventeenth Street and Pennsylvania Avenue, Northwest. The crêpe on the building is in mourning for the dead Lincoln. *National Archives.*

Hotel outlining plans for capturing the criminals. At the headquarters of Provost Marshal General Christopher C. Augur, Seventeenth Street and Pennsylvania Avenue, Northwest, testimony was being taken which fixed the assassination of the President on John Wilkes Booth.

Notices appeared, signed by General Augur, that a reward of ten thousand dollars would be paid "to the parties arresting the murderer of the President, Mr. Lincoln, and the assassin of the Secretary of State, Mr. Seward, and his son." To this was added a reward of twenty thousand dollars by the City Council of Washington. Eventually the rewards offered for the assassins reached a sum of more than two hundred thousand dollars. The belief that the Sewards would not recover proved to be untrue.

On the night of April 17 it seemed some of the money was due to be paid. Suspicion had rested on the heads of the Surratt family and officers were at their H Street home, searching it and questioning those present, when a man, clad in laboring clothes covered with mud, and bearing a pick-axe on his shoulders, knocked at their door. He was admitted and told to identify himself. He said he had called to inquire when Mrs. Surratt wished to have

him dig a ditch for her, since he intended to begin work early the next morning and did not want to disturb her at that hour. On further investigation, he turned out to be Lewis Payne, the assailant of Secretary Seward. No time was lost in "putting him in irons" (handcuffs). The whereabouts of John Surratt were unknown, but others in the house, including his mother, and sister Ann, were taken into custody.

That same day, a news item announced: "Ella Turner, the mistress of Booth . . . who attempted to commit suicide by taking chloroform at her sister's house . . . is, we understand, a young girl of about 22 or 23 years of age, whose proper name is Starr, and who is a native of Baltimore. Some years since, the sister married a very respectable typo, and went to Petersburg, Virginia, Ella going with them, but while there the matrimonial knot was dissolved, and the sisters, after sojourning in Richmond and other places south, made their way to this city." Ella's act resulted in all the inmates of the house "from the mistress to the cook, eight in all," being arrested, and her sister's confession that it was a place of prostitution.

The man-hunt for the assassin and his accomplices was the topic of conversation the

198

next day as people went to view the remains of Lincoln at the White House. A notice had been published that no one would be allowed to loiter there, so that "a jam may be avoided and order preserved." The first of the ceremonies preceding Lincoln's long funeral procession to the train awaiting the transportation of his body to Springfield, Illinois, had brought curious crowds from nearby cities and towns into Washington. At nine-thirty that morning, when the gates to the White House were thrown open, a solid mass of human beings, three or four deep, extended far along Pennsylvania Avenue. From the main entrance of the building, visitors passed through the Green Room into the East Room where Lincoln's body rested. From there they moved to a large open window and platform draped in mourning which were used as an exit. Each individual stood in line at least six hours in this last tribute to the martyred President.

The funeral on the following day was marked by the suspension of all business, the boom of minute guns and the tolling of bells. Long before noon, the streets, already filled with residents and visitors, began to run over with fresh arrivals. Everywhere were to be seen the various gatherings of associations, delegations and orders, preparing to join the procession which would accompany Lincoln's remains to the Capitol. Housetops were crammed with spectators and trees along the Avenue bore a perilously heavy burden of human beings. The Treasury colonnade was occupied by a patient throng holding tenure by "squatters' rights," and private and public grounds within sight of the line of march were filled to capacity.

Only those having tickets (about six hundred) were admitted to the White House for the funeral service. At noon President Johnson and the Cabinet, with the exception of Secretary Seward, entered the East Room. Mrs. Lincoln was not present, being too ill from nervous prostration and an incipient fever, brought on by excitement and sorrow. The two sons, Robert and Tad, were joined by relatives and other members of the household. All representatives of foreign governments, ambassadors, secretaries and attachés,

Arrest of Payne at the home of Mrs. Mary Surratt on H Street between Sixth and Seventh Streets, Northwest. The house is still standing but the front has been altered by removal of the stairway to the entrance on the second floor. *National Park Service.*

Annie Surratt, daughter of Mrs. Mary Surratt. How much she knew of Booth's plot is problematical. *National Archives.*

were present in "full court costume." Their high-collared and heavy gilt coats, their vests decorated with various orders, formed a glittering array among the sombre black garb worn by most persons in the room. The Reverend Phineas D. Gurley of the New York Avenue Presbyterian Church, where Lincoln had worshipped, conducted the funeral service. When the last words had been spoken and the coffin closed, it was carried by a detailed detachment of the Veteran Reserve Corps to the funeral carriage, draped in black, waiting at the entrance of the White House. Others in the room followed in their appointed order and took the places assigned to them in the cortège. Then began the journey down Pennsylvania Avenue to the Capitol. Lincoln's gray horse, saddled and with the martyred President's boots reversed in the stirrups, was led by a groom.

The funeral service at the White House was conducted by Phineas D. Gurley, pastor of the New York Avenue Presbyterian Church which the Lincoln family often attended. *National Park Service, Library of Congress.*

The funeral procession turns into Pennsylvania Avenue at Fifteenth Street, Northwest, on its way to the Capitol. *Library of Congress.*

Buildings along the route were heavily draped and photographs of Lincoln were displayed in many windows. Mottoes, too, such as "TREASON HAS DONE ITS WORST" and "THE NATION MOURNS A MARTYRED FATHER," hung in public places. An estimated thirty thousand took part in the procession, the Sons of Temperance being the largest civic organization represented. The great width of the Avenue allowed forty-four persons to walk abreast, or five carriages to drive side by side in the line of march. Nevertheless, the time occupied in passing a given point was one hour and thirty-five minutes.

About three o'clock, the first troops reached the north gate of the Capitol grounds. The entire space in front of the building and the steps to the entrance had been cleared of people and were well guarded. As the funeral carriage approached, a dirge was played by all the bands in unison while pallbearers alighted and carried the coffin to the rotunda, followed by the groups entitled to admission. A brief but impressive burial service, also

The funeral conveyance which carried the remains of Lincoln from the White House to the Capitol on April 19, 1865. *Library of Congress.*

The President's car becomes the funeral coach ready for the long journey back to Springfield, Illinois, with Lincoln's remains. *National Archives.*

read by Reverend Gurley, ended the ceremony. Baskets of flowers were then brought in and arranged around Lincoln's remains, left in charge of an Honor Guard for the night. Next morning the Guard was relieved by another detail and doors were thrown open to the public. Throughout the day a continuous stream of people, some thirty-five hundred per hour, went up the steps of the eastern entrance to the rotunda where the remains lay in state. They ascended a platform surrounding the catafalque, passed to the head of the coffin and on to the west exit of the building. At dark the doors were closed and the guards for the night took up their positions. About forty thousand viewed the martyred President's body at the Capitol. Had the weather not been so damp and chilly, the number probably would have been twice as large.

At the early hour of six A.M. on the Friday

following the assassination, the Cabinet, several senators and officers of the army, the Illinois delegations, and pallbearers, gathered in the rotunda for their farewell to Lincoln. The coffin was then closed and carried to the hearse which conveyed it to the railroad station. About the same time, the remains of little Willie Lincoln, the President's son who died in February 1862, and was buried in a vault at Oak Hill Cemetery, also arrived there for the journey to Springfield, Illinois.

The station, draped in mourning on the outside since the President's death, had early that day been similarly decorated within. All windows and door frames were draped and long heavy festoons hung from the cornice of the main waiting room. A large flag fringed with crêpe spread full length over the door leading to a platform with its railing wrapped in spans of black fabric. Above the gateway

202

to the train was an arch covered with mourning. The military, as soon as Lincoln's remains had passed, formed a line in the front and rear of the station, and a strong guard was placed at all approaches. Only high-ranking civilians, officers of the Army, Navy, and Marines, the delegations going with the train, representatives of the press, and passengers leaving for Philadelphia, were allowed to enter the building.

The coffins containing the bodies of Lincoln and his young son were placed in the second car from the rear. Originally built for the President and other dignitaries, the car con-

sisted of a parlor, sitting room and sleeping compartment. The windows had been hung with black curtains and the entire furniture was covered in black. Outside, along the top of each car, was a row of black and white rosettes, and a similar row with attached mourning extended around the car below the windows. The train was composed of eight cars, six of them being "double-deckers" of the Baltimore and Ohio Railroad. The last car, intended for the family and the Congressional Committee, was elaborately furnished and had a parlor, chamber, dining room and kitchen. The pilot engine and tender to pre-

Interior of Lincoln's funeral car, with the coffin and guard of honor. *National Park Service.*

cede the train, were heavily draped, all the brass was covered, and the flags fringed with mourning.

As the hour of departure of the train drew near, a committee of Senate and House members, an Illinois delegation, Robert Lincoln, several press correspondents, and others having tickets, boarded the cars. Mrs. Lincoln was too ill to leave her room, and, with her son Tad, remained at the White House until a later date. The pilot engine took its place some distance ahead, and at eight o'clock the signal to start was given. Simultaneously, the bells on all engines tolled and the train moved slowly from the station. Members of the Cabinet and other notables on the platform passed beyond the line of sentries to the rear of the depot and stood with heads uncovered until the train faded from view. Such were the scenes the thousands in Washington witnessed that week.

Meanwhile, the man-hunt had gone on for the assassins and those associated with what was believed to have been a great conspiracy against the heads of the Federal Government. Official notices that no information be published of arrests and investigations of culprits implicated in Lincoln's assassination, and the attempted murder of Secretary Seward and family, were given little attention when important news broke. Edward Spangler, a middle-aged, mild-looking stagehand at Ford's Theatre, accused of helping Wilkes Booth with arrangements inside the theatre; Samuel Arnold, trailed to Fort Monroe; and Michael O'Laughlin, picked up in Baltimore, had been taken into custody as conspirators in the plot. And on the day that Lincoln's remains left Washington, newspapers reported the capture of George Atzerodt at Germantown, Maryland. He had been brought to the city the night before in a special car attached to the ten o'clock train. Passengers had been prevented from leaving the train until he was taken to an omnibus seized at the station by military authorities for that purpose. He was rushed to a safe place of confinement to protect him from possible violence. This precaution only delayed his hanging.

204

Several days later the following appeared: "Circumstances which have come to the knowledge of the Government render it nearly certain that Booth's horse fell with him on Friday night, the 14th instant, and it is believed caused a fracture of one of his legs. It is also reported that he has divested himself of his moustache." But in the same edition the public read: "THE ASSASSINS—We hear considerable of interest in regard to the assassination plot and those concerned in it, which we refrain from publishing in accordance with the request of the authorities." Even that reprimand did not entirely gag the press for the testimony of many at Ford's Theatre on the night of Lincoln's assassination, which got into print, began to build up the evidence of the crime.

Comedy also enlivened a story that Wilkes Booth, wearing female apparel, had been seen entering a building in the vicinity of the Kirkwood House. Joe Hill, a well-known character, and formerly a watchman, went into a nearby restaurant and said that he had seen Booth, dressed as a woman, painted black, and wearing a Negro wig. Booth, walking on crutches, recognized Hill and muttered, "Joe, don't you say anything." The restaurant owner called a policeman who took Hill to the station house where the officer in charge greeted him with, "Drunk again, eh?" Having no intention of keeping such a pest in jail, the officer told him to go home and sober up. Nevertheless, Hill's story caused great excitement in the neighborhood and a house-to-house, roof-to-roof search was made by the Provost Guard, detectives, and police. The mob that had gathered to watch them was ordered to keep on the pavement next to the curb. About 8:30 P.M. they gradually dispersed for it had been definitely settled that there was nothing to Hill's story and the guard was being withdrawn.

Then came the startling news of the capture of Herold and the death of Booth twelve days after the assassination of Lincoln. Newspapers told how the two men had been tracked to the farm of Richard H. Garrett in Virginia by a detachment of the Sixteenth New York Cavalry, commanded by Lieutenant Edward

Edward Spangler, caught in the conspiracy web. *Library of Congress.*

Herold and the dead Booth are brought back to Washington. *National Park Service.*

P. Doherty. With them were Lieutenant Luther B. Baker and E. J. Conger, a former Lieutenant Colonel. All were sent southward by Colonel Lafayette C. Baker, cousin of the Lieutenant. The two fugitives had been found in a barn, surrounded, and told to come out. Herold did so, but Booth refused, and the barn was set on fire. A shot was heard, and Booth was dragged from the burning barn to the doorway of Garrett's house where he died. Belief that he was shot by Sergeant Boston Corbett is extremely questionable. Later evidence tends to prove that Booth shot himself rather than be captured and sent back to Washington where he knew he would be hanged.

It was past midnight when Herold and the body of Booth, conveyed in a sack made from a blanket, arrived at the Navy Yard after having been transferred from the steamer *John S. Ides* to a tugboat. At first, newspapers made no mention of the disposition of Booth's body and merely said that Herold had been lodged in a secure place. However, both had been transferred to the monitor *Montauk,* where Herold had been manacled, and Booth's corpse carried to the forward deck and a guard placed around it. "Very great curiosity prevails as to the disposition to be made of the remains of Booth," a later report said, "but it seems the authorities are not inclined to give his wretched carcass the honor of meeting public gaze and it probably will be deposited in whatever place promises the most utter obscurity for it. Yesterday a photographic view of the body was taken before it was removed from the *Monitor.*" A letter to the authorities suggested that it be buried under the sidewalk in front of Ford's Theatre directly below a flat stone of black marble inscribed, HERE LIES THE ASSASSIN, so that people could stamp their hatred of him on it. For years its hiding place was unknown to the public. Even Edwin Booth who, at the request of his mother, arrived in the city on April 28 hoping to obtain the body of his brother, was not informed of its whereabouts. Eventually it became known that it had been secretly buried under the stones of a cell in the old Penitentiary (called

"Stanton House" by the inmates), adjoining the Arsenal grounds.

Evidence had piled up. Dr. Mudd also had been arrested at his home in lower Maryland and brought to Washington. He was accused of having sheltered Booth and Herold, of attending to Booth's injured leg, and of aiding both fugitives in their flight southward. All the accused (eight in number) now were in chains on the monitors *Montauk* and *Saugus:* Spangler, O'Laughlin, Atzerodt, Herold, on the former; and Arnold, Paine, Mrs. Surratt, Dr. Mudd, on the latter. While minute guns fired throughout the afternoon of May 4, and government departments were closed in honor of Lincoln's funeral at Springfield, Colonel H. R. Burnett, Judge Advocate, prepared the cases against those arrested, and promised the clamoring public that they shortly would be brought to trial.

Four years of excitement in the city were being surpassed by events of the moment: "A thrill of horror was created in the community yesterday by the announcement in an Executive Proclamation that Jefferson Davis and others of his set had been ascertained to be the real movers in the assassination plot, and offering large rewards for their apprehension," declared one newspaper. "The deep-rooted aversion to Jefferson Davis as a cold-blooded huckster in men's lives for his own ambitious ends was intensified a thousandfold by the development of the fact that his unscrupulous intellect—for heart he has not—had guided the assassin's trigger and dagger, as well as the engines of wholesale murder. It was felt and expressed that the offense of Booth— horrible and unnatural as it was—bore no proportion of enormity compared to that of the originator who conceived it in his closet at Richmond. The tragedy-cracked player who did the deed, though deserving all the punishment a mortal can endure for his crime, was no such criminal as the cold-blooded politician who laid out his work. It needed, perhaps, some such culmination of infamy upon the name of the arch-traitor to make the people duly appreciate what treason is and what it leads to."

Offers of one hundred thousand dollars for

the arrest of Davis, and smaller sums for members of the "Little Confederate Cabinet" harbored in Canada, sought to link them with plots to poison Lincoln, send him infected clothing, and other "hellish designs upon his life." Their public denials of any complicity in the assassination plot, and the impossibility of arraigning them for trial in short order, did not delay the Government's intention to place a noose around the necks of all those in hand. Thus was set in motion, and evidence supplied to support it, a trial of the eight accused of murder, the original plot to kidnap Lincoln disappearing in the maze of testimony and information permitted to be recorded.

The prisoners were removed from the monitors to the old Penitentiary building where they were to be tried by a Military Commission. All were confined in a range of cells formerly occupied by female prisoners. They were manacled there, as in the courtroom, with this exception: in their cells they also were required to wear close-fitting padded hoods having holes for the eyes and mouth. These had been designed (so it was reported) to keep the prisoners from attempting suicide as Paine had done on the *Monitor* by butting his head against his prison walls. Each of the accused had an attendant constantly on duty. The prison fare was much the same as a

Prisoners, hooded and handcuffed, arriving at the Old Penitentiary Building, where they are to be tried, adjoining the arsenal grounds. *National Park Service.*

soldier's ration: meat, bread, and coffee, and occasionally beef soup, supplied three times a day in their separate cells.

On May 9, in a room arranged for the trial, the Military Commission disposed of preliminaries and gave the prisoners the opportunity of retaining counsel and conferring with them. The following morning they were arraigned on the charge and the specification, to which each pleaded not guilty. The charge read: "For maliciously, unlawfully and traitorously . . . combining, confederating and conspiring together with one John H. Surratt,

"The bullet with which our martyr President A. Lincoln was assassinated by J. W. Booth, as seen under a microscope," reads the caption under this macabre drawing published after the crime. *Library of Congress.*

John Wilkes Booth, Jefferson Davis, [the names of Confederate officials in Canada followed] and others unknown, to kill and murder . . . Abraham Lincoln . . . Andrew Johnson . . . William H. Seward . . . Ulysses S. Grant. . . ." Three days later, the courtroom was opened to the regular representatives of the press and others having passes.

As news of the proceedings got into circulation, the trial became a field day for the

208

public. Reports that Jeff Davis had been captured increased the excitement. Great crowds gathered in the Arsenal grounds to watch notables and the elite of Washington come and go. Perfumed ladies, gaily dressed, arrived and tittered, thrilled by the expectation of looking upon the little band of desperados. Even children were brought to see the show and gaze wild-eyed upon the "animals" in the dock. Ministers of the Gospel, Protestant and Catholic, also attended.

Everyone approached the building by passing through a strongly guarded street to an upper gate and a long line of sentinels reaching to the entrance. There, officers on duty checked passes and directed those permitted to attend the proceedings to the courtroom on the third floor. The room measured about forty by fifty feet and had four windows heavily grated. At the west end was the prisoners' dock, raised about one foot from the floor, and surrounded by a plain railing some four feet high. In front of it was the witness stand of the same height also enclosed by a railing. Another railing extended nearly the whole width of the room with just enough space for opening a large wooden door (studded with heavy bolts, and recently set in the wall) which led to the prison where the accused were confined. The court was seated around a long green baize-covered table on the north side of the room; official reporters of the commission and representatives of the press were at another table while counsel for the accused sat at tables in front of the prisoners' dock. Two upright stoves, a water cooler, some exceedingly hard-bottomed chairs, a tier of benches against the wall, and a score of well-patronized spittoons completed the furnishings of the room.

At each proceeding, the prisoners were brought in singly and taken to the raised seats in the dock, the accompanying soldier remaining close by. Atzerodt and Payne seemed to be the most unconcerned of the group. Payne directed a cool, impudent stare upon every person in the room. His bold eyes, prominent underjaw and athletic figure gave all the marks of a brazen, desperate villain, but not one capable of planning a deed of

Col. Clendenin   Brig.-Gen. Howe   Col. Tompkins   Maj.-Gen. Wallace   Maj.-Gen. Hunter   Brig.-Gen. Foster   Judge Bingham   Judge Holt
Brig.-Gen. Harris   Brig.-Gen. Ekin   Maj.-Gen. Kautz   Col. Burnett

The Military Commission engaged in the trial of the conspirators was composed of officers and civilians known for their loyalty to the United States Government. *National Archives.*

A strong guard was posted in front of the main entrance to the Old Penitentiary Building during the trial of the conspirators. *Library of Congress.*

cunning. He affected a rowdyish dress consisting of a close-fitting, collarless, blue woolen undershirt and pants of the same color and material. Atzerodt, dressed in a coarse suit of mixed gray, was the shortest of all and had the meanest face. His thickset shoulders indicated great physical strength. O'Laughlin, Arnold and Spangler were nervous and worried, especially the former, who looked pale and haggard. The full forehead and rather reflective face of Dr. Mudd seemed much out of place among the low type countenances of his fellows. Herold looked dirty in face and dress, his hair apparently uncombed at all times. Mrs. Surratt, wearing deep mourning and heavily veiled, appeared much depressed. That was the stage setting and the cast of the court drama enacted for the people in Washington at the beginning of summer, 1865.

Day after day, the court and spectators listened to the evidence building up the charge of murder. Reports of the part played by Jeff Davis and other Confederate leaders continued to come in. Prosecuting attorneys sought to connect every scrap of testimony relating to a possible conspiracy by them and those in custody. Witnesses were brought in from far and near to bolster up the case. Hot weather made the courtroom uncomfortable and many persons, including some of the prisoners, appeared in shirt-sleeves. Mrs. Surratt carried a fan in her hand but seldom used it. All windows and doors were left open and guards with glittering bayonets were posted at the exit leading to the prison cells.

Reporters for the press complained that at two P.M. the court returned from luncheon well fortified for further labors of the day, but newsmen, who lunched on the smell of the court's food, came back to their work with hungry faces. "Why can't somebody start an eating stand at the penitentiary building for the use of the reporters during these trials?" they asked in print. "The isolation of a set of men, who for no other crime than being connected with a daily paper, are held here eight or ten hours a day, a mile from an oyster or a cocktail, is terrible to think of." But they did not fare so ill as Lieutenant Alexander Lovett

who, while a detective, had aided in capturing Booth and Herold. Lovett was now a commissioned officer in the Veteran Reserve Corps and a witness at the trial. Returning to his quarters at Stone Hospital, he saw four persons jump from a hiding place in a grove and fire pistol shots in his direction. Fortunately, none took effect. The hospital guard immediately scoured the locality but were unable to run down the would-be assailants. It was not known whether the attack was made in revenge for Lovett's participation in capturing the fugitives, or for purposes of robbery.

In the midst of the excitement occasioned by the trial, Mrs. Lincoln, Tad, and Robert (who had returned from the funeral of his father and brother), said goodbye to Washington friends and departed for their home in Springfield, Illinois. President Johnson and his family, who were guests at the home of Representative Samuel Hooper of Massachusetts, continued to live there until the mansion could be re-decorated for their occupancy.

Washington was overcrowded with summer tourists, drawn to the city by the trial and the impending Grand Review of the Army of the Republic. It was estimated that the railroads brought in more than one hundred thousand persons for the two-day celebration of the Review. Barrooms were ordered closed but liquor was sold in the speak-easies of the day and on the outskirts of the city. Many visitors obtained passes, through Congressmen, to the trial, and the room was packed to suffocation. Honeymooners were there, including the gallant General George A. Custer and his beautiful bride who received much attention by fellow officers. At one time the crush of spectators was so great in the direction of the prisoners' dock that they interfered with bringing them in, and guards were forced to push back the crowd. Clerks, reporters, and others having legitimate business in the room were seriously inconvenienced by the jam of thrill-hunters, and it became necessary to enclose the space used by the court with a railing.

After a short session on the first day of the

Crowd gathering at the Capitol for the grand review of the national armies. The black crêpe and flag at halfmast are in memory of Lincoln, dead six weeks. *Library of Congress.*

Grand Review the court decided to adjourn for the entire period of the celebration. Band music during early parades of the military forces was heard by the prisoners, some of whom stood up to look out of the windows. Activities, and the interception of travel at certain uptown points, had diminished attendance at the trial, for which those concerned were duly thankful. The city was enjoying its first day of gayety since Lincoln's assassination.

At dawn people began gathering at the Capitol and along Pennsylvania Avenue where it would be favorable to view the parade. Countless visitors, unable to get accommodations in hotels, had spent the night in the open air. Cavalry patrols were posted along the route to control the crowd and keep the Avenue clear. Every window, porch and balcony, and many housetops, were occupied. On the intersecting streets, carriages were drawn up with men and boys perched upon their wheels, and horsemen rode about, not infrequently threatening life and limb in their furious search for advantageous positions. Policemen devoted most of their energies to prostitutes, pickpockets, house thieves, and strangers with counterfeit money. The Fire

Department removed the dust by watering the Avenue, thereby making it pleasant for the veterans marching over the route.

Stands erected in front of the White House were decorated with flags, flowers, and evergreens. One, reserved for President Johnson, General Grant, the Cabinet, heads of civil and military departments and the diplomatic corps, displayed the names of famous battles in which the troops had participated. Other stands bore suitable mottoes such as "CONNECTICUT GREETS ALL WHO BRAVELY FOUGHT, AND WEEPS FOR ALL WHO FELL." From the entrance of the Treasury Building the flag of the Treasury Guard Regiment was displayed, the lower portion tattered and torn—not by battle, but by the spur of Wilkes Booth's boot as he jumped from the box to the stage at Ford's Theatre on the night of the assassination. An attached placard stated this fact and the flag attracted much attention.

A deafening cheer that rolled along with increasing volume announced the approach of General William Tecumseh Sherman as he walked toward the main reviewing stand. With uncovered head, the General, followed by a few of his staff, passed quietly up into the stand and greeted those awaiting them. As the first cheer subsided a second and more deafening outburst heralded the arrival of the great hero General Grant, who removed his battle-worn hat and acknowledged the ovation before taking his place in the stand. President Johnson's appearance brought another expression of welcome from the crowd.

Promptly at nine A.M. the report of a cannon was heard and, at the Capitol, bugles sounded as troops moved into the procession starting from that point. Bands played, and on the Capitol steps school children sang "The Battle Cry of Freedom," "When Johnny Comes Marching Home," "Victory At Last,"

President Johnson, the Cabinet, and General Grant, await the passing of officers and troops in the reviewing stand, decorated with flags and the names of famous battles, fronting the White House. *National Archives.*

Public school children, on the Capitol steps, sing popular songs as troops move into line for the parade of the grand review. *Library of Congress.*

"Sweets from the Sweet" reads the caption on this old print, showing ladies presenting flowers to Sherman's color-bearers near the White House. *Library of Congress.*

and other appropriate pieces. General George G. Meade, leading with the Army of the Potomac, rode a few paces in advance of his staff, the column moving by companies closed in mass, with shortened intervals between regiments, brigades and divisions. Six ambulances, three abreast, followed each brigade. Generals who had become famous in the course of the war, and their loyal veterans, were greeted with cheers and the waving of flags as they passed along in the Grand Review.

Crowds in front of the White House were suddenly thrilled as a magnificent stallion dashed madly past the President's stand with the rider, General Custer, vainly striving to check the spirited animal. A large wreath hung upon the General's arm, his scabbard was empty, his saber held aloft in salute, and his long hair waved in the wind. People arose from their seats in breathless suspense that changed to applause at the horsemanship of the General as he checked the frightened stallion and gracefully rode back to the head of his column. After passing the reviewing stand, some of the generals dismounted and joined distinguished guests there. That evening, in honor of the occasion, the City Hall, crowned with a large star, was illuminated, and gas jets over the door of the west entrance displayed the name of Grant opposite that of Sherman, with the word UNION centered between them.

Early on the second day of the Review, a cannon boomed, bugles blew, and General Sherman's armies took up the line of march. Arrangements were much the same as on the preceding day. Multitudes swarmed the streets, stands in front of the White House were filled with celebrated guests and both the President and General Grant again received ovations upon their arrival. But at the Capitol only a few school children showed up to join in the event. "They seem to have got completely hoarse and worn out by their all-day exercises yesterday," explained the press.

General Sherman, accompanied by Major General Oliver O. Howard, whose empty sleeve reminded everyone of his war record,

rode a little in advance of the staff with bouquets in their hands, and their horses gaily decorated with flowers. At the start, a soldier of the Veteran Reserves Corps approached Sherman with another bouquet, but the General's horse shied and he motioned the soldier back. "Give it to Howard," shouted someone in the crowd, but he, too, with his single hand, could attend to little else than his curvetting steed, and the soldier made no further effort to dispose of his tribute.

Next in line came General John A. Logan, commanding the Army of Tennessee, riding a magnificent iron-gray charger. Swarthy, erect and muscular, Logan looked the beau ideal of the soldier and modestly acknowledged the cheers which greeted him as he rode along the Avenue. A banner stretched across from two residences, was inscribed "ALL HAIL OUR WESTERN HEROES," followed by the names of battles in which these troops had fought. An engineer brigade, composed of white and colored troops, armed with axes, picks, and spades, also marched in the procession.

"An hour before noon," one reporter observed, "the sun poured through the breezeless air with intense heat and the crowds on the pavement sought the shade. Perspiration streamed over the faces of the bronzed soldiers, but their steps lost none of their elasticity, and their lines moved on with the same even front. Flowers hung from the breasts of the officers and the necks of the gaily caparisoned horses, and roses bloomed in the muzzles of the guns. The bullet-torn flags, draped in mourning for the martyred President, spoke no less feelingly of the gallant dead sleeping all the way from the Ohio down through the winding valleys of Tennessee and Georgia; and looking on the serried ranks, one seemed to lapse into a dream filled with visions of Vicksburg, Chattanooga and Atlanta, and campfires stretching on through the South to the ocean."

With the Army of Georgia was the Zouave Regiment (Second New York), uniformed in blue trimmed with red, and wearing crimson skull caps with blue tassels. Only a few men remained of the splendid organization that

General Sherman's veterans marching along Pennsylvania Avenue on their way to the reviewing stand. *Library of Congress.*

Contrabands in the wake of Sherman's Army who were part of his "Flying Transportation Department" in the parade of the Grand Review. *National Archives.*

started out at the beginning of the war, and their depleted ranks added to the sympathetic interest attached to their torn colors. Following them was the celebrated "flying transportation department" of Sherman's army led by two Negro boys riding diminutive donkeys. Perched on the backs of some pack horses and mules were a number of chickens, while two or three cows, several goats and dogs, and one mule brought from the plantation of Jeff Davis, trailed along behind them. Rumor had it that all this "truck" had been taken from prominent rebels. The comic spectacle in the rear of the procession was greeted with shouts and laughter throughout the entire line of march.

215

President Johnson's private office at the White House. *Library of Congress.*

As generals dismounted after passing the reviewing stand, they took places beside other distinguished guests there, and the troops they commanded moved on to camps assigned to them in other parts of the city. When the last column gave the final salute before the President, the crowd rushed toward the stand for a closer view of the occupants. But the President, the Cabinet, General Grant, and others, after a few handclasps, went their separate ways and the Grand Review of the Armies of the Republic ended.

Visitors who remained in Washington until the next morning found the White House doors thrown open to the public for the first time since the assassination. Workmen were engaged in removing the catafalque and

drapes of mourning in the East Room. That day President Johnson took possession of the public offices in the building, occupying the room in the east wing of the second floor formerly used by Lincoln. The living quarters, however, were not ready for the Johnson family until a later date.

"The great crowd of strangers has not yet left us," commmented one reporter. Lingering in the capital for a resumption of the trial of the conspirators, they saw another review in June of the Sixth Corps of the Army of the Potomac, prevented by duty in Virginia from taking part in the Grand Review. Horse-cars operating between the White House and the old Penitentiary, where the conspirators were confined, were jammed from morning until night, and conductors were turning in to transportation companies twice the amount usually collected in fares. Continuation of the trial had brought thrill-seekers back to the courtroom anxious to gaze again upon the strange assortment of human beings awaiting the roundup of evidence and a verdict. O'Laughlin and Mrs. Surratt seemed more depressed than on the day of adjournment, the latter sitting in her corner "all in a heap" with eyes half closed and her face shaded by a palm leaf fan. For some reason the windows were kept closed and the atmosphere was pestilent.

The buzz of conversation from women spectators was almost irrepressible and drowned out the opening proceedings of the court until quiet was restored. After the noon recess, the "jam was more frightful than ever" —persons who had recuperated from the celebration of the. day before now packed the room to capacity. When the prisoners were brought in there was so much loud whispering and pointing of fingers that those charged with keeping order had difficulty in achieving it. On one occasion, spectators pushed forward as usual and the facetious remarks of women swarming about the dock caused Paine to blush with embarrassment.

Relic hunters, believing the trial near an end, were getting busy. Everything in the courtroom not bolted down was in danger of being carried away. According to one report, chairs, tables, etc., were beginning to suffer, "and it is possible that unless an Argus-eyed watch is kept upon the furniture, the court

Rare drawing of the conspiracy trial showing the eight prisoners (background) and members of the Military Commission trying them. *National Park Service.*

Witnesses and soldiers waiting for the execution of Mrs. Surratt, Payne, Herold, and Atzerodt (each in the order named) in the prison yard. *National Park Service.*

The Conspirators on the Scaffold, being Prepared for Execution.

will see it diminish visibly each day, and vanish altogether by the close of the trial. From eager glances bestowed by some of the lady visitors upon the hair of the prisoners, it is evident that they have a hankering for relics in that quarter; and as there is a rush each day to the prisoners' dock, as they come out and go in, it would not at any time surprise us to see some enterprising lady curiosity-hunter clipping away at the head of Payne, Herold, or some other of the long-haired prisoners, as they pass."

On the last day of May, Edwin Booth's appearance at the trial caused more furor than that of the prisoners. The likeness of the great tragedian to his brother John Wilkes was quite noticeable. Edwin had the same classical features and finely cut chin, but with a much more intellectual, gentle and thought-

ful face than John Wilkes possessed—so reporters described the silent man with a heavy heart. The purchase of Ford's Theatre, where these two Booths had played, by the Young Men's Christian Association was to be settled the following month, but the sale and plan to convert it into cheerful and comfortable club-like quarters (preserving Lincoln's private box, with a proper inscription) did not materialize. A few days later, military forces in charge of the theatre since the assassination were withdrawn and the keys of the building were turned over to James Gifford, chief carpenter and representative of John Ford. Both Ford and John Sleeper Clarke, brothers-in-law of the Booths, under guard for several weeks in the Old Capitol Prison, now were exonerated of all guilt in connection with Lincoln's assassination and released. This infuriated Secretary Stanton and the Government took over the property for use of the War Department.

Near the end of June, the packed courtroom and the prisoners listened in silence to the long and drawn-out closing argument of Judge John A. Bingham as he traced the course of events leading to the capture and arrest of the accused. "If this conspiracy was thus entered into by the accused," he said, "if John Wilkes Booth did kill and murder Abraham Lincoln in pursuance thereof, if Lewis Paine did, in pursuance of said conspir-acy, assault with intent to kill and murder William H. Seward, as stated, and if the several parties accused did commit the several acts alleged against them in the prosecution of said conspiracy, then, it is the law that all the parties to that conspiracy, whether present at the time of its execution or not, whether on trial before this court or not, are alike guilty of the several acts done by each in the execution of the common design."

A few more words, and the trial of the eight prisoners ended. It had been in session for over seven weeks. Only one action on the

TAKING THE BODIES DOWN FROM THE SCAFFOLD.

part of the Military Commission remained: the announcement of the findings and the verdicts imposed. There was little doubt in anyone's mind what that would be. While lightning flashed and thunder rolled through the darkness of a stormy night, the hooded and manacled prisoners awaited their doom. On the Fourth of July, they heard the booming of guns from the surrounding forts and the ringing of church bells throughout the city in celebration of the national holiday. Three days later, under a scorching afternoon sun, the trap of a scaffold in the Arsenal yard

was sprung and the bodies of Mrs. Surratt, Payne, Herold, and Atzerodt (each in the order named) writhed in mid-air until dead. They were buried in the Arsenal yard not far from the wall of the building separating them from the body of John Wilkes Booth, to await further disposition by families or friends. Dr. Mudd, Arnold, O'Laughlin (life), and Spangler (six years), were sentenced to prison on Dry Tortugas Island off the coast of Florida where O'Laughlin died of yellow fever. In time, the other three were pardoned by President Johnson. John Surratt

National Park Service

THE SURGEONS EXAMINING THE BODIES AFTER THE EXECUTION.

escaped to Rome, Italy, enlisted in the Pope's Zouaves under the name of John Watson, was recognized by a former Baltimore acquaintance while there, and two years after the crime was brought back to the United States for trial as one of Lincoln's assassins. The jury disagreed on the evidence presented that he was guilty of murder and his case was dropped. They did agree, however, that had

222

he been indicted for conspiracy to abduct Lincoln instead of conspiracy to murder him, they would have convicted him on the first ballot.

In his Message to Congress, when it convened the following December, President Johnson said: "It is not too much to ask, in the name of the whole people, that, on the one side, the plan of restoration shall proceed

Exciting scene in the old House of Representatives on the announcement of the passage of the amendment to the Constitution abolishing slavery forever. *Library of Congress.*

in conformity with a willingness to cast the disorders of the past into oblivion; and that on the other, the evidence of sincerity in the future maintenance of the Union shall be put beyond any doubt by the ratification of the proposed amendment to the Constitution, which provides for the abolition of slavery forever within the limits of our country. So long as the adoption of this amendment is de-layed, so long will doubt, and jealousy, and uncertainty prevail. This is the measure which will efface the sad memory of the past; this is the measure which will most certainly call population, and capital, and security to those parts of the Union that need them most. Indeed, it is not too much to ask of the states which are now resuming their places in the family of the Union to give this pledge of perpetual loyalty and peace. Until it is done, the past, however much we may desire it, will not be forgotten.

"The adoption of the amendment reunites us beyond all power of disruption. It heals the wound that is still imperfectly closed; it removes slavery, the element which has so long perplexed and divided the country; it makes of us once more a united people, renewed and strengthened, bound more than ever to mutual affection and support."

On December 18, 1865, the Thirteenth Amendment to the Constitution was ratified. In faraway Springfield, Illinois, the body of Abraham Lincoln lay entombed. The Union of the States had been preserved.

The coffin containing the remains of Mr. Abraham Lincoln. *National Park Service*.